NOV 0 5 2013

W9-BZW-456

1000
HOME DETAILS

1000
HOME DETAILS

A COMPLETE BOOK OF INSPIRING IDEAS TO IMPROVE HOME DECORATION

Editor: Francesc Zamora Mola

FIREFLY BOOKS

A FIREFLY BOOK

Published by Firefly Books Ltd. 2013

First printing

Publisher Cataloging-in-Publication Data (U.S.)

A CIP record for this title is available from the Library of Congress

Library and Archives Canada Cataloguing in Publication

A CIP record for this title is available from Library and Archives Canada

Published in the United States by
Firefly Books (U.S.) Inc.
P.O. Box 1338, Ellicott Station
Buffalo, New York 14205

Published in Canada by
Firefly Books Ltd.
50 Staples Avenue, Unit 1
Richmond Hill, Ontario L4B 0A7

Cover design: Erin R. Holmes/Soplari Design

Printed in China

Developed by
LOFT Publications
c/ Domènech, 7-9, 2º 1ª
08012 Barcelona, Spain
www.loftpublications.com

For Loft:
Editorial coordinator: Claudia Martínez Alonso
Editorial assistant: Ana Marques
Art director: Mireia Casanovas Soley
Editor: Francesc Zamora Mola
Text: Alejandra Muñoz Solano, Àlex Sánchez Vidiella, Irene Vidal Oliveras, Manel Gutiérrez (@mgutico)
Layout: Cristina Simó Perales, Sara Abril Abajo

INTRODUCTION

From the kitchen where we start our busy days to relaxing bedrooms and bathrooms, we want each space to reflect our personality. Outdoor spaces are extensions of our homes and therefore, the same rules should apply. The same depth of thought must be put into every one of these spaces. We certainly want our rooms to look stunning, but also utilitarian. Form and function in decorating are equally important, and every room should accommodate the ways the occupants live, entertain, work and relax. Pulling all the components together can be arduous, but it can also be very rewarding.

When it comes to decorating, everything counts, down to the last detail. It is a work in progress, and so a home is actually never "finished." It evolves over time reflecting trends, lifestyle and our own personal tastes. A good way to start out is with questions about function, mood and personality, the three main design considerations.

Before taking any action, put some thought into who will be using a particular room: adults, children, both? How will it function: as a place for entertaining, as a working area, as a retreat for relaxation? Some questions should be room specific. For instance, how many cooks use the kitchen? Or how many members of a family share a bathroom? Once you've ascertained how a room should function, focus on how you want it to feel and what sort of mood you wish to create: cheerful, relaxing, dramatic? There is nothing better than vibrant colors to create a cheerful room where the sun seems to always shine. On the other hand, a neutral color palette tends to suit calm personalities. Using eye-catching furnishings sparingly or mixed with diverse styles can achieve a dramatic modern look.

Beyond a well-planned selection of furniture — which will probably constitute a major part of your budget — accessories, artwork, window treatments and linens will complement and bring in the final touches, reflecting your personality. Are you attracted to vintage style? Traditional, rustic cottage, French country, contemporary, eclectic? Each decorating style comes with its own characteristics and can fit in any room of the house, whether it's the living and dining room, the kitchen, the bedroom or the bathroom.

Vintage style showcases items of the past, some of which you can repurpose by transforming them into fresh home accents. Traditional styles are made up of classic furnishings often in formal arrangements. The key is to achieve a traditional style without looking dated. Rustic cottage is practical and comfortable, with soft colors and natural materials. It provides a space with a casual character whether it is a seaside retreat, a mountain refuge or a penthouse apartment in the city. Floral patterns, antique furnishings and gilded accents are characteristics of French country. With its casual elegance and homey comfort, this style pays homage to the south of France. More than just a palette of neutral colors and clean lines, modern style seeks a balance between sleek open spaces and comfort, avoiding an excess of accessories.

Regardless of style, each room should be looked at with specific attention. The living room is probably the most lived-in room of a home and might present a bit of a challenge since it often incorporates a dining area, and sometimes even a workspace. A sofa, some chairs, oversized floor pillows for lounging and several side tables can fashion a comfortable living room. Small gestures such as extra pillows, flower arrangements and scented candles create instant ambience.

The kitchen is more than just a cooking and eating place. If space allows for an island, it can be a nucleus for socializing. It needs to be, nonetheless, a functional utilitarian room with tough materials, good lighting, integrated appliances and cabinetry with convenient features.

While the living area and the kitchen are spaces suitable for socializing, the bedroom is a private space. It is a room where one can express their most personal tastes. Decorating a bedroom for kids is fun, but can be intimidating, while a master suite with a bathroom invites a luxurious treatment.

If your bathroom is frequented by the whole family, it's more important than ever to plan carefully. Along with choosing the proper materials, you'll want plenty of storage for towels and supplies.

When designing an outdoor space, it should be looked at in the same way as an interior room. By paying the same attention to detail as you would when decorating your home, you will create a seamless transition between interior and exterior, so that the style feels unified throughout the home.

Whether you are redecorating or moving into an empty new home, and regardless of the mood you want to create and the style you are inspired by, you can achieve an amazing one-of-a-kind look that reflects your personality. Get inspired! Put together color schemes using paints, wallpapers and fabrics from the wide variety of materials and finishes available. Get ideas on how to arrange furniture and how to use decorating accessories for every room of your home.

0001 Straight lines and curves applied in appropriate proportions stand out in a living room with balanced character. If plain surfaces and angles predominate on the sofa and armchairs, their best accessories are a spare table and round cushions, and a pouf instead of a stool.

0002 The lively tones in these sofas are common in the Italian Adrenalina brand, which expresses the essence of contemporary life in its designs without abandoning comfort. There is no need to fear bright shapes and colors if we want to offer a good dose of originality.

0003 Just as the living room furniture distribution is crucial, we also have to take into account the balance of weights. In this case, a solid and sturdy sofa is balanced by the accessories — a table and an armchair with a sleek, austere style of relative lightness. (Arketipo)

0004 An armchair with simple lines, upholstered in leather and with a chromed steel base, is very suitable for building a minimalist and frank style, as well as being both comfortable and ergonomic. (Domus by Arketipo)

0005 A living room atmosphere can be renewed without too much investment. Throw pillows are an essential detail on a sofa and can be changed at whim. These pleasant fabrics give a new life to the quilted back classical sofa.

0006 Poufs, footrests and ottomans are all ideal for obtaining additional space in a living room in a very practical way. With a pouf, the imprecise roundness and the lightness of the filling are features that make adaptability its best quality.

0007 A living room is an ideal space in which to create a reading nook. Making use of natural lighting as much as possible, use a low, wide armchair with a high reclining back. This is perfectly complemented with a matching side table.

0001

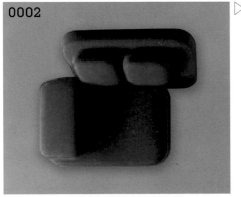

0002

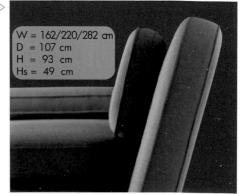

W = 162/220/282 cm
D = 107 cm
H = 93 cm
Hs = 49 cm

0003

0004

0007

0005

0006

0008 Absolute white is a tempting color option because of its freshness, purity and brightness. It is also a demanding and powerful color, since every touch of color in accent pieces captures attention.

0009 Unexpected materials and bright colors are a perfect combination if we are looking to avoid monotony and surprise ourselves every day. In this case, the wall pattern and chair's originality bring an undeniable vitality to the living room.

0010 This curule seat adds some colonial flair to this living room. The delicately carved floral detail echoes the floral patterns of the pillows on the couch. Although not particularly comfortable to sit on for a long time, a curule seat makes a good accent piece.

0011 In this rural living room two groups of color can be appreciated: the deep terracotta tones of the fabric on the furniture harmonize with the floor and contrast with the wall's wood, the curtain and the light-toned carpet. Thus a cozy, comfortable and casual environment is created.

0012

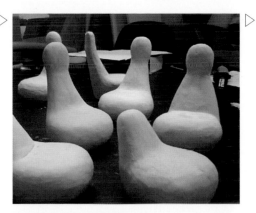

0013

0014

0012 Oppo (the armchair) and Puppa (the hassock) are two designs that give a lot of personality to a room thanks to their wide range of colors and their varying configurations: one armchair only, with an accessory bedside table and footrest ... (Puppa and Oppo by Blå Station)

0013 If we have a large space available in the house's common areas, the sofa's dimensions can be taken to the limits of magnificence: a very wide sofa in several positions, with or without a back, different sized cushions and a multiplicity of uses. (Arketipo)

0014 The space underneath the stairs is commonly used as a wardrobe, pantry or even as a powder room for guests. In some cases it is possible to make the most of this protected corner to create a warm and cozy place to relax, with a built-in sofa.

0015 The thread-bare look of some materials can be charming. A leather sofa's shabby, worn-out leather, with its history and use on display, is the center of this living room's rural and naked style.

0016 Unexpected details needn't be exclusive to daring and alternative design choices. In this relaxed family living room, a mirror in the armchair's arms is a pleasant surprise.

0017 Armless armchairs offer a lavish feel: the back is wider, the seat is deeper and the upholstery is thick and extremely fluffy. In this case, a neutral color makes the legs stand out slightly, reminiscent of 1950s style.

0018 Animal leather patterns have come back into fashion. For a chic and modern style, vibrant colors like this royal purple are daring when combined with a black and white zebra-patterned carpet.

0019

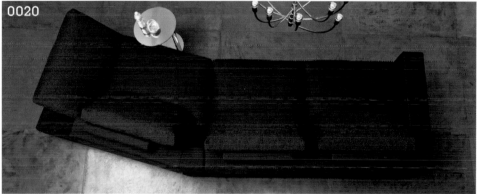

0020

0021

0019 The combination of black and white is striking. It has a chic, urban look and is never old-fashioned. In a living room, glossy materials like this sofa's metallic base, amplify the sophistication of the contrast of black and white.

0020 Where technology and comfort meet, this sofa's cushions can be adjusted on different axes and inclinations to suit those seated. (Arquetipo)

0021 It is very easy to make use of a living room corner with charm and grace. These window-seat cushions can go with an aromatherapy set, a vase of flowers or a book that invites us to enjoy it with natural light.

0022 Some sofas' accessory units include central divans or heightened footrests that can be used instead of a central table, since their size and height are adapted to sitting, lying down, resting feet or placing a tray of food.

0023 The arrangement of the seating in a living room is an important consideration. In this case, natural light floods the sofa from the back, and a separate seating area has been created with the placement of swiveling armchairs and side tables over a warm and delicate carpet. (Arketipo)

0024 This design has been conceived as a modular structure in which two elements, a pouf and a glossy stack of shelves, can join together with the sofa in different positions. The freedom and mobility of the set lets the space be renewed and adjusted, eliminating all restrictions. (Peanut B by Bonaldo)

0025 The genius of good design can be seen in the successful transformation of this deck chair from relaxed and informal, to an elegant and sophisticated piece, through a careful selection of materials and the refinement of composition lines. (Arketipo)

0026 The combination of two settees illuminated by a single light source creates an alternative reading and meeting corner, to the traditional group of sofa and side table. In this case, this arrangement takes advantage of natural light and a wall with attractive motifs.

0027 Red velvet is a symbol of exuberant and sensual luxury. A cherry chaise lounge is theatrical, dramatic and mischievous all at the same time. This type of furniture remains a classic with its silky tactility and winding shapes, just like the bold color.

0022

0023

0024

0025

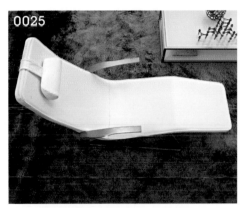

0027

0026

0028 It is essential to get sofas and armchairs of the best design in terms of comfort and durability. Poufs, stools and ottomans, offer more play and plasticity as occasional and decorative seating.

0029 The grid that constitutes this chair brings a fresh feel to the living room because it reminds us of the wicker and rattan furniture used in gardens and terraces. A feeling of warmth can be achieved with the addition of a blanket and a leather or light-colored cushion.

0030 Consider complementing a neutral-toned living room with multi-colored and brightly patterned fabric. With their cheerful combination of flowers and stripes, these floor pillows evoke a playful and casual feel.

0031 Simple geometric shapes reveal good craftwork while maintaining their pure nature. A wooden stool offers a spot of warmth in this cold-floored space and represents the organic world, in addition to being practical and long lasting.

0028

0029

0030

0031

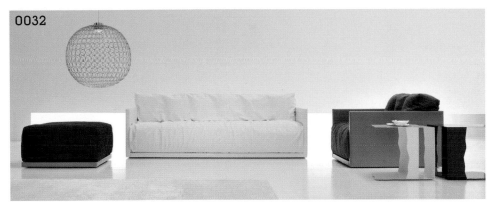

0032

0033

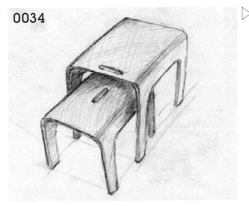

0034

0035

0032 An effective way to achieve a minimalist feel in the living room, is to distribute color to each piece of furniture, and maintain a single neutral tone on the walls. In this way, the areas of color are restricted in an orderly and measured way.

0033 In addition to the high collar and fluffy filling, this seat's upholstery contributes to its comfort. A wide-striped fabric gives the armchair presence and invites relaxation. The small details of a few pops of red in the painting, the pattern on the cushion and in the wood's mahogany tone are subtle but impactful.

0034 A key element to this molded wood stool's design, is a wide space between the top and the legs. This allows it to be versatile in its functions: stool or spare table, it can be combined in its three sizes and stacked when not in use. (Bimbo by Blå Station)

0035 The matte sand tones of the upholstery and the table contrast nicely with the shiny copper finish of the lamp. In addition to the range of colors and finishes, adding a side table the same height as the sofa helps create a feeling of stability and sense of homogeny.

0036 An isolated seat will not look out of place in a living room if we consider the context that the shape, tonality and finish suggests. A chair that evokes antique dining rooms with a tall straight embellished back and re-fined upholstery, looks marvelous against a backdrop of classic books and encyclopedias.

0037 Seats with simple arms and medium backs can easily be placed in any space in the house, in order to obtain additional seating.

0038 The Muuto Brand reinterprets traditional Nordic design by putting a twist on everyday objects. This sofa has a steel base, but a wooden frame. The dark color stands out in a predominantly white living room with excellent lighting. (Anderssen & Voll for Muuto)

0039

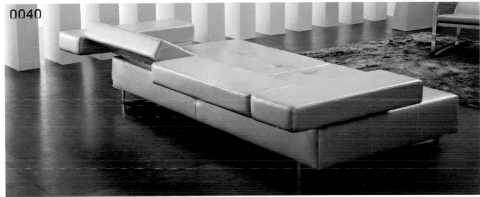

0040

0041

0039 Smaller homes can benefit from multi-functional creations like this pleasant settee: untie the laces found on the back, and the seat is transformed into a floor-level futon and a stool with storage space. (Tutumo by Kaori Shiina for Bonaldo)

0040 This sofa's flattened shape is the structural base of an original modular system that allows the angle of the seat back to change. In this way, different positions can be adopted on the same sofa. (Arketipo)

0041 The high-quality of the fabrics and fillings used in this furniture allows the original design to materialize as it was conceived. For this reason, each armchair has specific technical requirements, whether covered in cloth or leather, or filled with feather goose down or polyurethane foam. (Minotti)

0042 When graced with a striking architectural element, such as this floating staircase, a home's beauty can be enhanced with the careful placement of an artistic item, such as a sculpture, a suitably sized mirror, a group of candles, a leafy plant or a seat of contemporary design on the landing or under the stairs.

0043 The choice of colors for the living room can be posed as a superposition of alternate plans. In this case, two colors follow one another, the green and the white, to create a feeling of depth.

0044 The charm of a piece of furniture's finish and detail can lay in their imperfection or wear. Furnishings that do not hide the years of their use provide great personality in a living room.

0042

0043

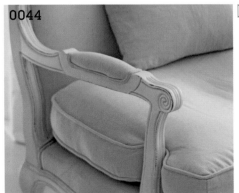

0044

0045

0046

0047

0045 The windows and spectacular view offer a sublime background to the dominant white in this room, complemented by subtle touches of black and metal. The delicately cushioned and smooth-lined sofas are in keeping with the carpet and curtains' ethereal feeling.

0046 This light chair embodies modern elegance and innovative design. The angles and slope of the back guarantee comfort, and with targeted lighting, interesting shadows can be cast on the surrounding space.

0047 The combination of different styles gives rise to a space with its own personality: an armchair's rustic and rural feel with its smooth material and lines, warms up the industrial sideboard with straight lines and metallic luster.

0048 A great way to update and revive an inherited or secondhand armchair is to reupholster it in a daring color that contrasts greatly with the wood. In this example, the bright blue of the armchair leather parallels the colors in the tile.

0049 For a traditional style we can opt for a flawless combination: classic furniture and a Persian rug. The fabric's saturated colors and abstract motifs correspond to the baroque ornamental engraving and the dark, brilliant and ornate wood.

0050 Antique furniture can adapt to be used in a contemporary space if we dare to experiment. Taking into consideration the pattern that the sofa dictates, incorporate subtle and original details, like reused materials and a touch of color.

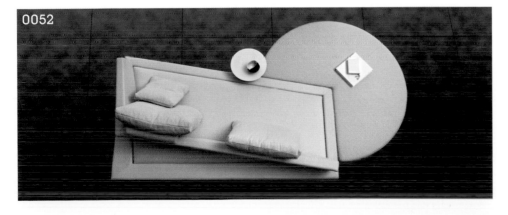

0051 The sculptural character of this chair incorporates natural details into a prism design that projects dynamism. The polyurethane foam smooths the geometric lines and offers us an armchair that we can also pull up to the dining room table.

0052 This avant-garde design is striking but it can give the impression of impracticality for the necessities of everyday life. However, in addition to being original, this sofa's unconventional geometry has been designed for providing comfort and versatility.

0053 This seat has an external structure made of ash wood which functions as a protective barrier for the user: the back's extension around the sides creates an isolated space that conserves heat and provides greater privacy and comfort. (Koja by Blå Station)

0054 The optimal armchair design should incorporate a wide support for the head, an inclined back and of course, a footrest. In this example, the black leather is elegant and is highlighted by the colored carpet.

0055 On the coldest days, furniture that has been upholstered in warm and textural materials can make optimal use of the heat that an adjacent fireplace provides. These ideal chairs for this warm corner in front of the hearth are low, with wide back and inclining seat.

0053

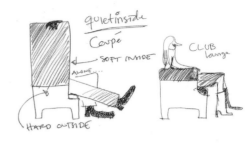

0054

0055

0056

0057

0058

0056 This armchair's design is suggestive of past eras with a high back, and angles and edges that are slightly dropped. The metallic base gives lightness and modernity to the solid volume. (Coley by Minotti)

0057 In spite of blacks inherent elegance and distinction, it is not easy to incorporate into a home's interior. A way to make it work in a living room is to make the most of the natural shine of the finish of the leather or wood the furniture is made of, and complement it with transparent and reflective elements.

0058 Traditionally shaped sofas can establish a sobriety in a living room that can be tempered with carefully chosen upholstery, curtains, wall decorations and other more versatile and transitory accessories, like vases and cushions.

0059

0060

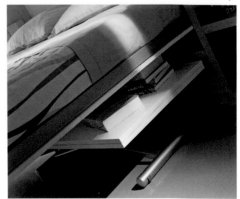

0061

0062

0063

0064

0059 Wall systems that combine stacks of shelves with open or closed compartments for storage or display, can incorporate the rest of the living room's furniture as well, taking maximum advantage of the available space.

0060 This design in particular allows a small living room to be converted into a guest room. In addition to the structure's design, it is important to choose a type of fabric for the sofa bed and the pouf that has a neutral motif, which is as functional in the communal space as in the private one.

0061 L-shaped sofas, with their modular or extended arm supports and incorporated chaise lounges, are suitable for homes of variable affluence, and easily serve both needs of an individual, as well as larger groups of people.

0062 Storage space incorporated into a sofa could not be more useful, especially when the sofa can also be folded out into a bed. It is a convenient place for storing pillows, sheets and blankets, ready to be used at any given time.

0063 The balance between elegance and comfort in a living room does not only depend on the sofa's shape and upholstery. Other accessories, like cushions and carpets, offer opportunities to create a stunning, yet cozy, intimate space.

0064 Swivel armchairs can be ideal in the living room, especially when their design aims to achieve the highest levels of comfort through the use of mechanisms for regulating angle and height, as well as adapting their resistance according to their user's weight and current position.

0065 Varied tactile qualities and strong colors are key to the décor of this living room. Contrasting colors have been chosen for the sofa and carpet, in silky and textured materials, that stand out amongst the accessories and white furniture scattered here and there.

0065

0066 A couple of occasional tables side by side can house all those things you want to have close at hand. They provide surface space for lamps, books, candles and drinks.

0067 There are a lot of ways you can use pallets and turn them into something creative and useful. This is an extremely simple coffee table that was made with a recycled pallet and casters.

0068 What can we do with a pallet? Even though they are not made of good quality wood, pallets can make for an interesting piece of furniture if you are looking for a rustic style.

0069 This is another example of a pallet's versatile use. This one, turned into a coffee table, provides the living room with an industrial touch. It harmonizes with the fireplace mantle and contrasts with the rug and the blankets on the sofa.

0070 Salvaged wood often has a beautiful aged grain and varied colors that imbue a piece of furniture with a rich patina and a lot of character.

0071 The several small tables in this living room ensure that there is adequate room for drinks and can even be used as additional seating when necessary.

0072 This stunning coffee table is only a couple of shipping pallets and a can of paint away. In this case, stacking two white painted pallets brings the table to a more useful height.

0073 Repurposing old suitcases and trunks allow for many creative combinations. Whether singled out to shine as a focal piece or stacked to form small tables or room accents, these items once used for traveling are a popular decorating trick.

0074 The form of this low coffee table seems to be inspired by pallet design. The table is made more practical by replacing the widely-spaced boards with a solid surface.

0075 An ottoman or upholstered bench can be used as an occasional table if it is firm enough. Have it match the sofa or curtains for a unified décor, while making good use of a versatile piece of furniture.

0076 Wood is still the material of choice in furniture making. In this case, a side table combines a modern design with the natural look of untreated wood.

0077 Tray tables are inspired by low Moroccan tea tables. This type of table is versatile, functional, movable and takes up very little space. Depending on the space available, you can set up a pair combining different colors and sizes.

0074

0075

0076

0077

0078

0079

0080

0081

0078 The use of recycled materials in furniture making is a popular design trend. Made of salvaged pieces of wood in different sizes and finishes, this coffee table and stool are unique pieces that add special character to the space they are used in.

0079 In most cases, trunks are tall enough to serve as a coffee table. Moreover, they can make for additional storage

0080 Inspired by Moroccan tray tables, the design of this side table features folding legs and a removable top. Excellent as accent furniture, it comes in handy as a place to set down a drink at a party and can easily be put away.

0081 While the occasional table is not a dominating piece of furniture, its style needs to fit with that of the room it is used in. This wood and steel table can be a perfect accessory in classically styled rooms.

0082 The simple design of this table will complement any décor: interior or exterior, rustic or modern. The reclaimed wood top and the steel frame give the table a sturdy quality.

0083 Yellow is a daring color, however, it can give the room a dynamic or relaxing feel depending on its hue and the amount it is used. A pair of small yellow tables will give a pleasant and sophisticated touch, and even more so if they accompany dark colored furniture.

0084 A small folding table at one end of a sofa provides an ideal solution to a room of limited space and creates a casual sitting area.

0085 A matching table and stool made of recycled wood with a steel frame complement the rustic look of the kitchen. The combination creates an industrial, loft-like atmosphere.

0086

0087

0088

0086 This brushed steel three legged occasional table is an interpretation of the popular wood version. It features a round top with a riveted edge that gives the piece an interesting industrial look. The overall design transcends periods and styles, becoming a one-of-a-kind piece.

0087 This side table — part of the sofa design — serves two purposes: it is an armrest and it doubles as a storage unit where you can keep books, blankets or anything you want to have close at hand when you are sitting on the sofa.

0088 New trends in furniture design have encouraged designers to think out of the box and produce unique furniture pieces using recycled parts of other items. For instance, this hand-made table has bicycle wheels.

0089 An ottoman or a pouf is a versatile piece of furniture. It can double as a footrest or an impromptu table. They also offer a fun way to add color, pattern and texture to a space.

0090 This small low table fits nicely in the simple interior that has a strong connection with the outside. The design of the table is plain just like the room, whose décor seems to focus on geometric forms. The spherical lampshade adds contrast both in shape and color.

0091 Set up a pane of glass on trestles for an improvised table instead of an ordinary piece of furniture. It is easy and budget-friendly!

0092 This coffee table is actually composed of two parts that are similar in shape but differ in height and color. Their flexible designs allow for many combinations.

0093 Tray tables can be used in many different ways. This characteristic has more relevance if, in addition, the tray includes handles that facilitate its handling.

0094 A wooden coffee table with a glass top is the focal point of this classically styled sitting area. Its light and airy design has a transparent element that helps to open up the look of the room.

0095 Although black and white is a minimalist choice for a contemporary living room, pairing these two colors with a third will intensify the contrast. The proportions in the use of the different shades should be so that one is the general color and the other two are accent colors.

0096 Rustic interior decoration is characterized by carved or turned items such as this low turned-leg table, which in combination with the animal hide emphasizes the desired effect.

0097 Bring in a vintage piece of furniture to start arranging your retro looking living room! This side table with tapered legs dictates the overall design of the room.

0098 The beauty of this coffee table lies in the interplay of smooth curvy lines and sharp edges. White is a good choice to bring a cool and airy feel to a room.

0099 This round metal side table, with a shelf to stack magazines or any other items, is ideal for rooms with space limitations. The brushed finish harmonizes with the black leather armchair.

0100 Minimal and lightweight, this plastic side table is suitable for interior or exterior use. Combined with a retro-looking couch and a brightly colored rug, the design of the table adds to the fresh clean feel of the living room.

0101 The use of polymer in the production of furniture offers great advantages. The result is durable and functional items, available in an unlimited range of shapes and colors.

0102 This table is modeled after a typical Moroccan tray table. This simplified interpretation features a wooden frame characterized by its straight lines and a powder-coated steel tray.

0103 Pierantonio Bonacina's Lario table features chrome steel legs and a mirrored top framed by a wicker band, which allows the table to be used as a tray.

0104 Side tables are very useful because of the minimal space they take up. Normally located against the wall, lamps and decorating items can be displayed on them.

0105 The Bresson coffee table by Minotti is available in two shapes: circular and square. The elegant laser cut forms and black and nickel finishes give the tables an elegant and unique appearance.

0106 This luxury design is distinguished by materials of optimum quality and a made-to-measure functionality. This furniture frame is rigid but its inner arrangement can be personalized according to the interests of the user. It has been devised to house the latest entertainment and multimedia technologies. (Alivar's Off-shore System)

0107 For a hanging shelf stack, the type of wall determines the appropriate style. The roughness of the stone and concrete are complemented by a small, primarily decorative, simple, single-ledged stack of shelves, enhanced by rustic materials, like roughly sanded wood.

0108 The four geometric figures of this shelving unit produce a rhythm of patterns that transform an often static and normal piece of furniture into one of dynamic, original aesthetics and variable functionality.

0109 Bookshelves and other objects that are not built into the wall can have other functions in addition to organization and display, like this tall bookcase that has an incorporated lamp.

0110 These floating shelves are simple with clean lines, and make great use of space in the smaller living room. Furthermore, they support all types of objects and blend well with the existing walls and windows, without clashing with other furniture or obstructing the entry of natural light.

0111 This modular system has been made up from several four-sided units with varying divisions inside that give rise to multiple combinations. Available in three different modules, these structures can be used horizontally, vertically or joined together.

0106

0107

0108

0109

0110

0111

0112

0113

14

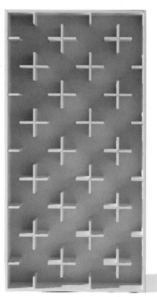

Structure

	White
	Grey-beige

0115

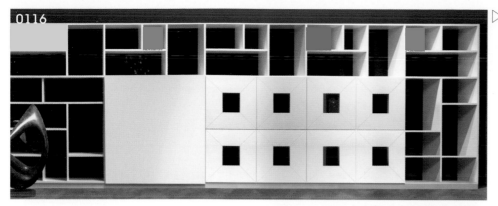

0112 Modular libraries allow as many of their components to be assembled together as are desired. This open modular design creates a visual effect if it is placed in front of a colored wall and can also separate spaces without obstructing general vision or isolating the rooms completely. (Ciacci Kreaty Cover)

0113 Shelving units often don't have doors. In this case though, some modules are closed while others are left open, giving the option of concealing less decorative objects. There is also the visual impact of the combination of different wood tones for the structure and for the doors.

0114 This shelving unit's design has the distinction of being able to house books of different heights. The crosses can carry less capacity than a normal bookshelf, but all sizes of books fit, besides being an attractive and very light arrangement thanks to the voids created by the composition of the structure. (Archetype Target)

0115 The installation of glass doors protects and frames the decorative elements placed inside a niche. In this case, the striking color of the doors guides the eye toward the sculptures that it shelters.

0116 Besana's Concerto bookcase is a modular composition of open shelves and cabinets. Housing books and displaying objects can transcend the ordinary and become creative when the bookcase has an eye-catching arrangement.

0117 Integrating removable desks onto the shelving unit is a way of taking advantage of the space and the furniture's functionality. A variety of inner compartments allows for the organization and availability of necessary objects in the working area.

0118 Bookshelves that have widely spaced shelves are great for displaying objects of different sizes and purpose. The wide design and the honey tone of the wood complement its basic lines.

0119 Light colors and smooth textures help to keep this built-in from appearing over-designed. The photographs and other objects placed in the shelves become the focal point when they rest on a white shelf.

0120 Using a limited color palette on the walls, the built-in and the sofa allows the displayed objects and other decorative elements in this living room, like the colors and prints on the throw pillows, to shine.

0121 Sequence is a modular shelving system designed by Patricia Urquiola for Molteni&C. Its geometric design embraces concepts of symmetry and asymmetry through the free positioning of dividers in solid or punctured steel.

0119

0120

0121

0122

0123

0124

0125

0122 Several small niches of the same size in a wall can create a focal point. They are part of a final composition that can include decorative items enhanced with spotlights, for instance.

0123 In this piece of furniture, enclosed storage is alternated with open storage, intended for decorative display. The smooth honey wood of the structural modules is combined with easy opening flap doors in taupe.

0124 A period chair adds a relaxing feel to an interior space with white-washed walls. The niche gives an indication of the massive construction of the wall, which contrasts with the delicate wicker caning on the chair's back.

0125 Shelving space below a pass-through can be used for displaying any kind of object, but also can come in handy as a bar between the kitchen and the living area, where guests can gather for drinks and snacks, while chatting with the cook.

0126

0127

0128

0129

0130

0131

0132

0126 This refinished antique bookcase gets a new life in a home among items of other periods including an Art Deco desk, a modern area rug and contemporary photographic artwork. It is all tied together with a neutral color palette: dark stained wood flooring and ceiling beams and off-white walls.

0127 Built-in shelves are easy to integrate in the décor of a room since they are part of the architecture. The front of the shelves can either be flush with the face of the wall and not alter the shape of the room or can project into the space, creating a focal point.

0128 These libraries are made of acrylic stone, a composite, biodegradable material of great strength and durability. Its quality and appearance remain unaltered by the passage of time because it is a waterproof material, neither absorbent nor porous. (Alivar's Wavy)

0129 You can create storage space with built-ins in the underused nooks of a room. They can serve as ledges for displaying artwork as an alternative to hanging pictures from the wall, or they can serve as a console table behind a couch.

0130 The Pass system is representative of Molteni&C's experience in the multimedia furnishing sector. This wall-mounted unit, available in various configurations, has colored glass doors that allow remote control signals to pass through.

0131 More decorative than utilitarian, these shelves would not stand the weight of books or heavy items, but adorned with a few objects they can make a great room divider. When using shelves in this way, keep in mind that if the unit is taller than 6 feet, one of its sides needs to be attached to a wall.

0132 Although generally made for displaying china, a built in cabinet can provide a handy display space for tableware, books and knickknacks. A good advantage of built-ins is that they offer storage space without taking up floor area.

0133 Sideboards in a dining room can serve several functions: from the display of vases with flowers, pictures, mirrors and other decorative accessories, to more practical uses like storing linens or china.

0134 The use of color integrates several of this desk's components. In this case, the upper part of the wall is white while the lower part almost merges with the tonality of the table. The accessories and colors show prominently thanks to the delineation of the space.

0135 The originality of this item of furniture is rooted in its similarity with homemade do-it-yourself craftwork. The repurposed filing boxes as drawers and the choice of pastel shades transmit this feeling.

0136 Small details, like an antique lock or silver-plated knobs on the wide drawers, give a delicate touch to a high, robust and large capacity item of furniture that can hold all the tableware, adornments and works of art for the table.

0137 A console table can break up a large space and separate it into different functions, for instance a living room and a dining room. A nice console table can also hide the back of a sofa, which are often plain and not particularly attractive.

0138 Rustic French design gives a stylized quality to this side table. The large hinges and bolts are a special touch to this piece, that in addition to its interesting height has generous space for storage.

0139 An inventive hutch above the sideboard, in the same quality and style of wood, is not only functional, it also marks out areas in a lively colored wall that frame the objects that are on display in it.

0140 The open spaces in the wooden and iron or steel items of furniture make them lighter and more pleasant. This dining room allows us to appreciate the floor's texture and sideboard design, just like the change of direction, horizontal or vertical, in the grain of the wood.

0133

0134

0135

0136

0137

0138

0139

0140

0141 Using a combination of different styles is an interesting decor choice. In this example, classically designed furniture with very wavy lines, stylized and curved legs, ornate applications and an elegant light tone contrast nicely with the wicker seat.

0142 A dark-stained wood chest of drawers from the first half of the 20th century integrates nicely into a room with a ceramic tile floor and natural stone walls. Regardless of the style and size, remember that you'll have a chest for a long time and you might want to move it around, so choose wisely.

0143 A very ornate heavy wooden item of furniture is an excellent accessory for formal and distinguished spaces: the wood's dark color contrasts with the red accents, and the carving gives it a delicate yet imposing presence.

0144 This green apple sideboard echoes the elegant lines of an 18th-century Genovese style chest. Bold colors and the high-gloss lacquer finish combined with antique-inspired furnishings, add some zest to a modern interior.

0141

0142

0143

0144

0145

0146

0147

0148

0149

0150

0145 A side table with drawers and a matching mirror makes a perfect vanity table. This simple, rustic and clean lined example will brighten a stone or log cabin interior.

0146 This trunk is an exceptional accent piece that lends old-world style to a home. A trunk can be used as a table, but depending on its condition and how attractive the exterior is, it can stand on its own. It can also be used as a bench, while providing additional storage space.

0147 Aesthetic details are printed onto the metallic structured furniture, and small wheels allow its movement and functional character, defining a very modern and practical industrial style

0148 This table's simple and basic structure doesn't demand attention and allows the texture of the wooden floor and qualitites of the stone wall to be appreciated.

0149 The white finish, simple forms and straight-forward functionality are the main features of Scandinavian furniture design, and combine very well with basic accessories of the same color.

0150 The light color of the accessories — boxes and candles — stands out amid the harmonious and matte color range shared by the wall, floor and furniture.

0151

0152

0153

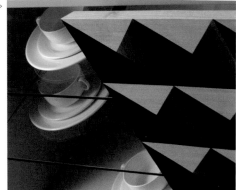

0154

0155

0156

0157

0151 A console table can complete a seating area, adding storage and display space. Lamps make good decoration items on a console table, but you must think of how you are going to deal with unsightly dangling cords.

0152 Fratelli Spinelli is an Italian furniture company known for its transformable systems composed of modular entertainment centers that can be turned into convenient bedroom furniture, including a bed. The daytime compositions are completed with a TV console and plenty of storage.

0153 This Italian design's sliding doors are a marriage of a mastery of handicraft and avant-garde design. The decorative pattern's triangular edges fully accentuate the wood's qualities. (Artex de Besana)

0154 With a wooden base and chromed metal legs, this sideboard's body is notable because the pyramidal form of its modules reflects different light intensities on each face. (Prisma de Besana)

0155 Sobriety and exquisiteness are embodied in the compact and sturdy structure of this furniture, fabricated with a shiny lacquered material for the doors and the drawers, and with walnut wood in the details.

0156 A beautiful console table such as this 17th-century walnut piece makes an elegant focal point in this large room with a high ceiling. Highly decorative items like this should be allowed to shine on their own, and not be crowded by other furniture.

0157 The special design of some sideboards is better appreciated if we use them as space dividers — in halls, dining rooms or living rooms — instead of setting them against the wall. In this way, their fronts and corners can be appreciated by all.

0158 Patterned curtains enliven large rooms. The floral pattern of the curtains and the throw pillows harmonize with the blue-green color of the walls and floor, and animates the room.

0159 Roller blinds are a practical and efficient solution to control the amount of light that comes into a room.

0160 Large windows, balcony doors and bedroom windows are parts of the room that, just like an upholstered piece of furniture, offer the chance to dress up a room, while framing the views to the outside.

0161 Curtains perform important functions in a room, filtering light and providing privacy. This makes them an important decorative element and consequently, it is important to include them in the room design.

0162 Tasseled tiebacks are an elegant way of keeping draperies secured to one side. They come in a wide range of designs and are a nice detail.

0163 Due to their low opacity, sheer fabrics let enough light enter a space without sacrificing privacy.

0164 Curtains don't have to be boring, quite the opposite. They can be used in any kind of setting, whether modern, classical or rustic.

0165 Glass screens are an optimum decorative and functional solution to separate a space without building walls, with the added advantage of allowing light to travel through.

0166 Vertical blinds respond to lighting needs and privacy. Especially recommended for large windows or patio doors, the pivoting system that controls the position of the blinds filters light as needed.

0167 Matching drapes and throw pillows create a well-balanced appearance and are a great touch.

0160

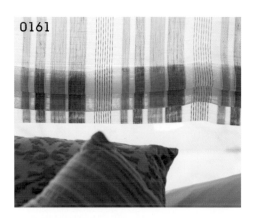

0161

0162

0163

0164

0165

0166

0167

0168 Fireplaces go unused at certain times of the year. One way of taking advantage of a fireplace in warmer seasons is to place stones and candles with harmonious textures and colors on the inside.

0169 The structure of this fireplace and chimney are reminiscent of the roof and frieze's classical style. These clean lines are mirrored in the geometric design of the colorful carpet.

0170 This fireplace is the focal point of this dining room. The floral relief and spotless white finish provide elegance to this classically styled fireplace that relies on modern technology.

0171 Books look very nice in the firebox when it is not in use. Other options include flowers, leaves and dry branches, decorative logs, mirrors, photographs, etc.

0168

0169

0170

0171

0172

0173

0174

0175

0172 Prefabricated wood-burning stoves can be added to any room in the house and they are made to the measure. They are most efficient because they produce the largest quantity of heat for the least amount of energy. The elevated body and trap-doors eliminate annoyances like smoke and ash.

0173 The structure and arrangement of the fireplace can serve as an invitation for a reinvigorating rest. Elevated upon a rise, this fireplace makes for a perfect welcoming and personal reading corner, in this rural home.

0174 Freestanding modern fireplaces provide a spacious and light feeling in a room, given that they are not a heavy element anchored to the floor and wall, but are instead suspended delicately from their chimney. In an environment where bland colors and light browns preside, the ergonomic form and dark material make this fireplace a showpiece.

0175 Brick and stone are materials that guarantee longevity for a fireplace, since they do not crack or split at high temperatures. The casually stacked wood and soot on the mantle gives a warm and cozy feel to the dining room.

0176 The biomass fuel that is used in pellet stoves can be stored externally, or is sometimes located in a hopper that is usually in the upper part of the stove. It is possible to put fragrances and essential oils into the deposit to create an aromatherapy effect throughout house.

0177 The pellet heaters have got an automatic function system that allows us to program the fire's duration, strength and temperature. In this way a constant and controlled temperature is maintained in all of the house's environments.

0178 Modern fireplaces perfectly balance the age-old tradition of the hearth as center of the home, with technology and innovative design. In this case, the frame has nickel steel cladding and the woodshed and fire screen are built in.

0179

0180

0181

0179 An ideal solution for enhanced heat distribution is to choose a double-sided fireplace. The fire functions at the same time as a boundary and transition between the different rooms of the house, which take advantage of the flames' heat in equal measure.

0180 Gas stoves and fireplaces offer two essential advantages for a stressful and busy life: on the one hand they offer the highest efficiency; and on the other hand, they eliminate complications like cleaning ash, and the purchase and the storage of firewood or any other fuel.

0181 With the metal box chimney's modern design built-in, the firewood's combustion is fully exploited and we can appreciate the pleasant contrast between the metal and wood. The stack of logs in a very vertical space gives a special touch to the set.

0182

0183

0184

0185

0186

0187

0182 One of the highlights of having a fireplace, and lighting a fire is the color, shape, scent and pleasant texture of firewood. When piled tidily firewood looks good in urban and refined environments.

0183 The face of this fireplace has a steel frame coated with bronze powder; the aesthetic can be adapted to different housing styles, from a modern loft to a cozy rural home.

0184 Storing your firewood indoors needn't be an eyesore, and in fact can have real appeal. Stacked neatly in a built-in or freestanding shelf, or under a nearby bench, it can be a striking decorative element.

0185 The new MCZ range offers both pellet and traditional woodburning stoves. This design's simple and clean lines are made possible due to detachable handles that can be put away when not being used.

0186 While classical designs make the most of the surround facing as a shelf, contemporary designs often have no mantel, and the facing is flush or only slightly raised from the wall. In this contemporary example, the ceramic surround facing extends horizontally along the wall, echoing the width of the firebox. Ceramics are some of the most interesting materials to use in surround facing, because they allow for creative decorative details and are available in several colors.

0187 The proximity of flammable objects such as carpets and books is not an obstacle for enjoying the fireplace, because the modern designs provide safety tools like security doors, ledges and brass or marble edgings to avoid accidents.

0188 Wallpaper is a simple and budget-friendly way to renew the look of a room. The texture of this wall resembles cracked clay. It emphasizes the fireplace and enhances the framed artwork.

0189 The antiqued gold embossed finish of this texturally based wallpaper provides the living room with a touch of luxury.

0190 Nature motifs can be found in many wallpaper designs. In this case, elegant mossy tones create a patina that serves as a rich backdrop to an Asian antique.

0191 The choice of materials imparts style as much as accessories. The renaissance touch and the deep ornamental relief in this ceiling define in great measure this space's style.

0192 These hand-painted ceramics are handcrafted masterpieces that enrich the space. The traditional design in deep blue and yellow above the varnished white are dynamic.

0193 These flagstones are made of pigmented cement and offer countless geometric floral models, with reliefs and drawings that imitate antique or modern mosaics. Some manufacturers offer a personalized design service by means of which the colors can be chosen.

0194 The combination of opposite styles — classic and modern — is materialized in this space. The wall's classic aura with frescoes and the mirror's carved frame contrasts the chair's modern design.

0195 A mural with palace motifs are appropriate for a room of great distinction and elegance, in which other elements, like the ceiling, the curtains and the lamps, have to coexist aesthetically.

0196 Rustic elements, like stone walls, have become a star tendency in the decoration of interiors. In this way warmth is achieved in spaces where tradition and modernity cohabit. In this living room, the Sagar stove stands out, made of steel and powder-coated in black.

0197 This damask pattern is created with the repeated image of a Damascus plant. The silvery sheen of this pistachio version harmonizes with the chrome light fixture and chair.

0194

0195

0196

0197

0198

0199

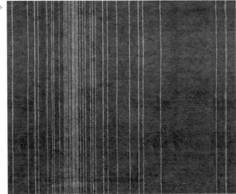

0200

0201

0202

0203

0204

0205

0198 Inspired by the dandelion, this original print combines audacious colors and black outlines. This popular design is applied to wallpaper and upholstery fabrics.

0199 The most important characteristic of this rug is the effortless combination of a modern aesthetic with impeccable handicraft. It is designed and made to last, embracing the natural beauty of the material.

0200 The décor of this living room harmoniously combines the different materials of the table's tempered glass, the various textures of the leather sofa and the interesting weave of the rug.

0201 The modern and geometric fireplace and acrylic furniture blend amicably with the organic nature of the wicker furniture and lush foliage in this living room.

0202 The design of this wallpaper is inspired by vintage Indian silk saris. The golden and washed-out burgundy stripes are printed using a photogravure technique.

0203 A fireplace set into a stone-clad wall has a clean modern look in this living room. This steel fireplace surround incorporates storage for firewood.

0204 The design of this living room spotlights the mixture of materials. The oak stool, the wool and silk rug, the painted sideboard and the concrete walls are a well-balanced combination.

0205 Audacious urban spaces allow for the stark combination of white and black because they carry the impression of modernity and distinction at the same time. In this case, the pattern on the wall is the primary focus and, therefore, the furnishings and accessories are subdued in their lines and textures.

0206 An eclectic atmosphere can be easily achieved through the careful selection of a few key elements, like motley printed wallpaper and elaborate candelabras adorned with hanging glass crystals.

0207 These spheres, embellished with seeds and silver pellets are placed in a golden bowl on a wooden table, and result in a harmonious arrangement of layers that combine natural and metallic elements.

0208 There is a certain honor in not concealing the passage of time and allowing the age of the material to be show with grace and dignity. These accessories boast an ennobling aged effect in the silverware's rust and the lamp's worn-out base.

0209 A critical consideration in floral arrangements is the relationship between the type of flowers and the vessel that contains them. In this case, springy and rounded flowers rest inside the spherical vase that, in addition, leaves the stems in view.

0210 Fabrics can radically transform spaces through texture and color's expressive capacity. In this case the natural fibers and brown smoke tone of the throw pillows with a brightly colored accent, transmit a rustic and homely feeling.

0211

0212

0214

0213

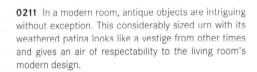

0211 In a modern room, antique objects are intriguing without exception. This considerably sized urn with its weathered patina looks like a vestige from other times and gives an air of respectability to the living room's modern design.

0212 When an object is repurposed, its qualities can be strengthened in its new application. This wooden carving that may have been on the lintel of an entrance hall or an adornment on a piece of furniture, now decorates a wall in harmony with the range of the other accessories' colors.

0213 Some isolated accessories are subtly reminiscent of times past. These zoomorphic candlesticks and the sculpture of an angelic baby above the sideboard combine well with the antique furniture and the brown and cream-toned palette.

0214 Another way to play with sizes is progression: the union of three identical accessories of growing dimensions — small, medium and large — is a configuration for decorative accessories that can be placed on living room furniture.

0215 A birdcage converted into a vase for a dried leaf arrangment is a good example of how to exploit the latent versatility of all types of objects. Separated from its context and used for functions that are not its own, the accessory is remarkable for its originality.

0216 A way of creating balance when decorating is to play with the size of comparable objects. A large bowl paired with smaller bowls similar in shape and color is an example of how to achieve a clean style with uniform lines and shapes.

0217 Excellent results can be achieved when a monochromatic scheme is applied to a room's heavier elements, with the addition of some details in a contrasting color that combine well with the base tone, but stand out. In this living room, the accessories in blue envigorate the space.

0218

0219

0220

0221

0218 These simple forms are enriched by the contrast of the materials. We can protect a candle with a glass cloche that is reminiscent of a butter dish. Its cylindrical form is mirrored by the height of the small round and deep toned wooden table.

0219 The matte finish of the rug, and the glossy finish of the leather pillows juxtapose the natural texture of the base material against the fine texture of the processed product.

0220 This living room's accessories create a dynamic feeling. Aside from the cohesive color palette, the circular incisions in the bottles on the table are echoed in the hypnotizing effect of the picture's concentric circles, creating a feeling of movement.

0221 When we choose a style for our living room, we have to pay attention to each element in order to achieve a coherent atmosphere. In this case a modern and urban style has been complemented by the high contrast black and white chevron-pattered rug

0222 To creatively and economically decorate a wall, opt for photographs. You can frame them in any style that suits your decor aesthetic.

0223 Wall decoration with photographs is very common. For a touch of originality, establish a visual relationship between the type of image and the frame, like aged black and white photos in a thick wooden antiqued frame.

0224 Made of wood, or wrapped in leather or fabric, trunks fulfill their primary purpose of storing clothes and other objects. In the living room they come in handy for the storage of throws, extra pillows and the like, while serving as a striking coffee table.

0225

0226

0227

0228

0229

0225 While frames are a typical and more lasting way of displaying photographs and artwork, other more creative options exist that allow us to easily change out photos, post cards and even notes that we want have close by.

0226 In a living room where light and pastel tones dominate, use accessories to accent the room. In addition to jars with flowers, other options are airtight transparent containers with sand, herbs or spices.

0227 Wall mounted magazine racks allow us to organize and display books, magazines and other printed materials. Important considerations are the type of wall the rack is being mounted on, as well as the capacity of the unit. Many are metallic, easy to clean and durable.

0228 Candles in a living room create a warm and intimate atmosphere. Even if they remain unlit, a candle's color, texture and shape turn it into a lasting and practical accessory. Furthermore, candlescapes can be created with the addition of candelabras and other accessories like shells, mirrors and flowers.

0229 The orchid is one of the most appreciated flowers in interior decoration because of the range of striking colors they come in, to the uniqueness of its shape. When incorporating an orchid into your interior design, try recreating the plant's natural conditions, taking into account lighting and moisture.

0230 To visually expand a living room and enhance the quality of the light, use a mirror. Reflection transforms a room. Make sure that the frame works with the decorating style of the room.

0231 If the tones that dominate a room are black and white, choose accents that go well with both but that bring some zest to the room, such as the sparkling crystal chandelier and ornately framed mirror in this example.

0232 The abundance of squares in different functional objects are a focal point in this living room. The geometry emphasizes with the material's raw yet elegant character; the cushion's soft, warm leather contrasts with the cold and smooth reflective quality of the mirrors.

0233

0234

0235

0236

0233 Metal and glass pieces make excellent décor items in living rooms of muted and dark tones. Sheen, just like transparency and reflection, produce an interesting visual effect of color and light.

0234 A living room is a space that allows a greater combination of styles and cultures. These large vases with floral and calligraphic decorations recall ancient civilizations with their exotic and aged feel.

0235 This mirror reflects the ceiling's moldings, adding visual interest to the room. The mirror also brightens up the room by reflecting light.

0236 As an alternative to a traditional rectangular mirror, this composition of several round mirrors reflects the exterior in an unusual and geometric way. The disorganized configuration is balanced with the classic style of the furniture and walls.

0237 Hanging ornaments from tree branches seems like something we would do in children's rooms, but it is perfectly feasible in living rooms as demonstrated in this example.

0238 In a living room with rural or garden style furniture, a throw pillow in striped fabric is ideal. For a bit of playfulness, and to vary the look, vary the direction of the fabric's lines, with some vertical and others horizontal.

0239 Cheerful, casual and vibrantly colored, these cushions bring dynamism to this living room. Classic tartan patterns are reinvented with brilliant color combinations. Of course, if you opt for patterned cushions, choose a solid cloth for the sofa.

0237

0238

0239

0240

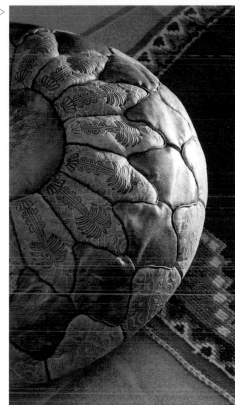

0241

0240 Moroccan or Turkish style textiles feature intricate and multicolored embroidery. Choose one design, or mix different ones for a more exuberant and exotic ambience.

0241 Furry blankets and throw pillows add an irresistably tactile element to a room, and in combination with the warmth they provide, makes them perfect to cuddle up in.

0242 Don't be afraid of choosing a multitude of different patterns, textures and motifs in the fabrics and textiles used in a living room. Provided they complement each other, and the general decor of the room, it won't necessarily overwhelm.

0243 A great way to ensure that mixed fabrics can work together, is to maintain a chromatic or style relationship. In this case, the color and graphic image on one of the pillows harmonizes well with the furry blanket of similar tones.

0244 The charm of neutral tones can add even more value as a decorative element with the addition of texture. A touch of color is always welcome, and even more so if it comes accompanied by a rich texture.

0245 A luxe environment has been created in this rural setting with the choice of fabrics similar in tone, weight and texture for the rug and upholstered furnishings.

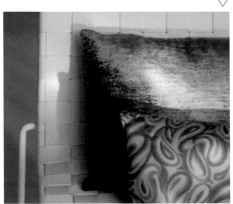

0246

0247

0248

0249

0246 White and neutral tones combine very well with natural materials like wood and handcrafted fabrics. A monochromatic palette, for all of the living room's decorations and accessories — lamps, candles, flowers and cushions — creates a balanced and harmonious atmosphere.

0247 Large vases can be placed on the floor of the living room, in the foyer and hallways. Made of ceramic, metal or acrylic, these vessels can hold flowers and ornamental leaves.

0248 Lime green and pink are usually used together in children's rooms or at parties because of the cheerful combination of colors. This color palette in a living room is, without a doubt, a successful attempt to fill the room with energy.

0249 Colorful pillows add a touch of color to an otherwise bland sofa. Changing out throw pillows are the easiest but most impactful way to restyle the atmosphere of a room.

0250

0251

0252

0253

0255

0254

0250 When an animal motif is used in a children's room, farm animals are the most common choice. In living rooms, others prevail. Flowers, birds, butterflies, elk, deer, and other wild, Nordic and African savannah animals are common.

0251 Monochromatic color schemes convey serenity. Start with the main color and add some color variations in the accessories and décor objects.

0252 The embroidered and quilted fabrics in these pillows create an interesting texture and are pleasant to the touch.

0253 Textiles with smooth color patterns and muted drawings are ideal for living rooms decorated in a French country style, in which white dominates and is combined with light and pastel shades. Accessorize with rustic furnishings, such as trunks, ceramic jars, chests and natural fabrics, to further cement the look.

0254 Embroidered pillows with floral designs and pastel colors are a good trick for decorating a "shabby chic" style room. Use them in spaces that mix antique and modern elements to establish an elegant and welcoming atmosphere.

0255 When combining cushions of different fabrics, take into consideration texture, color and pattern. Use this trick to add a colorful touch to your living space.

0256 To brighten a living room and add an artistic flair, use pillows with graphic patterns.

0256

0257 The harmonious and minimalist design of this Rhythm light fixture (designed by Arik Levy for Vibia) has multiple configurations thanks to a pivoting system allowing the undulating movement of its "ribs."

0258 Nigel Coates' Angel Falls for Terzani is an original sculptural light. Suspended from a large LED lighting fixture, crystal angels seem to be in dancing in the air. A dramatic piece like this can be an accent in a room decorated with ornate Victorian elements, or can stand alone as the centerpiece of a room.

0259 For a special touch, and to enliven a plain white wall, a brightly colored lamp like this one is a great solution. Composed of a metallic frame with an elastic, removable and washable cover in many choices of color, it can be a wall, ceiling or hanging lamp. (Muse de Axo Light)

0257

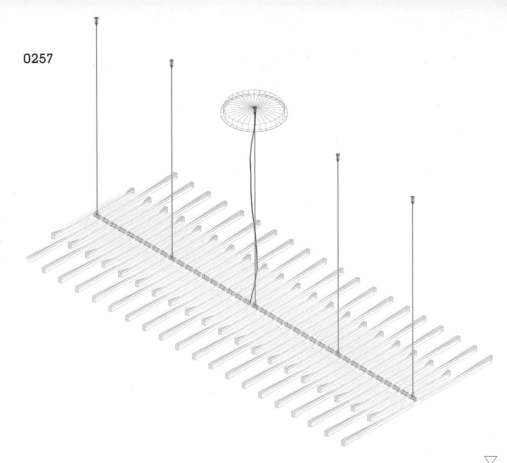

0258

0260 In dining rooms with high ceilings, the most effective chandelier will be large and dramatic. In this case, a light fixture with hanging lights provides the space with the necessary light and adds a decorative touch.

0261 The combination of hand-worked wire, crystal drops, and lace cover give this light fixture a kitschy feel and gives a casual and relaxed touch to the living room.

0262 This is a new version of the Bubi lamp designed in 2001 and launched in the market by Pandul. The original shape was inspired by the designer's grandchild's sombrero. The cover has a chrome finish and the differently colored cables create a playful atmosphere.

0263 This hanging lamp stands out for its original cluster shape with cylindrical shades. Despite the number of bulbs, the amount of light is surprisingly not excessive, as it is filtered through the rice paper shades.

0260

0261

0262

0263

0264

0265

0266

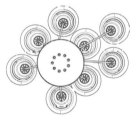

0267

0264 This hanging fixture's uniqueness comes from its ingenious arrangement. Identical lamps of different diameters fit inside each other like in "Matryoshkas" or, Russian nesting dolls.

0265 The unusual but striking large black sockets gives this fixture an exceptional and timeless quality.

0266 In libraries and offices where focused light is required, spotlights are the ideal solution. In this case, these low-energy LED lights are adjustable, with the ability to direct light wherever needed.

0267 Despite this low-energy table lamp's thin shape, it provides sufficient light with an LED tube with a high efficiency heat dissipator. The design is distinctly minimalist and has high functionality. The light is suspended by two fine, adjustable cables.

0268 This chandelier is the room's main feature, not only for its magnitude, but also for the combination of textures in the arm's ornate weathered metal, the pleated shades and the glass and crystal that reflect the color of the walls.

0269 A chandelier-type fixture has grandiosity and elaborate design that bestow elegance upon a rustic space — in this case, the rough brick ceiling. The melted wax effect and light bulb's resemblance to a flame shape recall these lamps medieval origin.

0270 These chandeliers provide a solemn elegance and serve as an ideal complement in classic living rooms, with friezes and ornaments on their ceilings. The hanging adornments' transparent material sparkles at different angles in the light's reflection.

0271 With the aim of transforming a space through the small details, the combination of shades of different sizes and colors on this classic chandelier provides color and a contemporary and personal touch to a classic piece.

0272 To create a warm and familiar atmosphere, avoid typical matching light fixtures and choose different lamps or chandeliers for each area of the living and dining rooms. This creates small lit environments with exceptional lamps, and plays with two disparate styles.

0273 Crystal drops are an element of chandelier design that recall the refinement and pomp of a palace. They can adapt to different applications in the home, adorning table lamps and ceiling-mounted fixtures.

0274 A wall-mounted light fixture, placed high on the wall, draws the eyes upward. This method of enlarging the sense of space in a room works exceptionally well in a dining room.

0275 Metal is an interesting material for lamp shades, as it offers several colors, like brass or nickel, and finishes, such as shiny, matte or aged. In this example, an ornamental design has been cut out of the smooth copper surface, allowing light to filter outward, as well as down.

0276 The VP1 Flowerpot light, designed by Verment Panton in 1964, is characterized by the simplicity of its lines. It has become a classic design thanks to its distinguishable form.

0277 The configuration of this ceiling lamp is dramatic and eyecatching. The light bulbs on each of the triangular faces of the metallic icosahedron emit a direct light that, like the lighting in an actors dressing room, provide an urban, cabaret touch.

0274

0275

0276

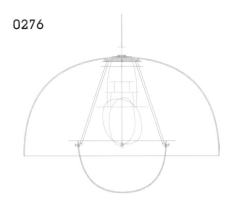

0277

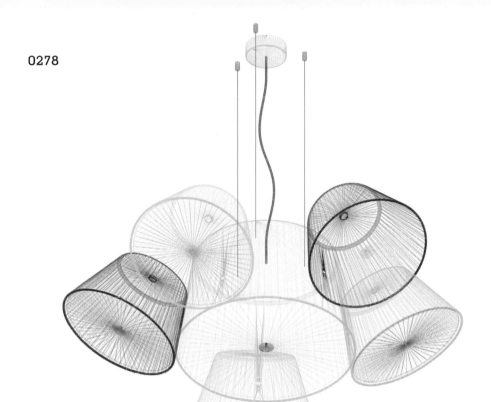

0278 Marset's Tam Tam lamps are characterized by repetition, and by the archetypical shades that cover a number of lights shining in different directions.

0279 The ceiling lamp is one of the most pivotal elements in establishing a room's general style, as its position has a significant visual impact. The choice of a fixture with a distinctive aesthetic is decisive and governs the space.

0280 In a living room with a double-height ceiling and wooden saddle beams, the gaze is naturally directed upward. In these rooms it is convenient to choose a lamp that meshes with the style both in the living and dining rooms.

0281 These fixtures have been designed to create a cozy environment around a table. The seams are folded outward around the edge of each panel that shape the screens' modular box. (Hood light fixture for Ateljé Lyktan)

0280

0281

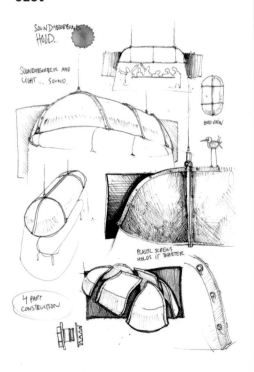

0282

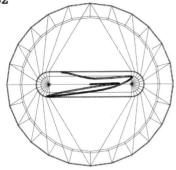

0283

0284

0282 With a shape inspired by machinery, these ceiling lamps for the dining room are made of blown glass. The bulky thickness causes a pleasant shade of light and the wide mouth is ideal for long tables. (Size de Belux)

0283 Increasing reliance on technology can result in a greater appreciation for the calm sense of well-being that is associated with nature. There is a particular appeal to handcrafted objects and the activities that create them. The presence of a hand knitted lampshade imbues this room with warmth.

0284 The white lampshades in this dining room, together with white walls and curtains, contribute to the quality of the light in the room. It also allows the wooden ceiling and beams to stand out, and their textures are better appreciated.

0285 We can obtain a subtle harmony between several key pieces of a room: the ceiling lamps radiate a bright but transparent color and share tones with the accessories, all over a light, neutral canvas.

0286 La Belle is a lamp that emits a pleasant, diffuse light, providing an enjoyable atmosphere. A white polyethylene drum and a transparent diffuser combines to create a light fixture that is not likely to go unnoticed.

0285

0286

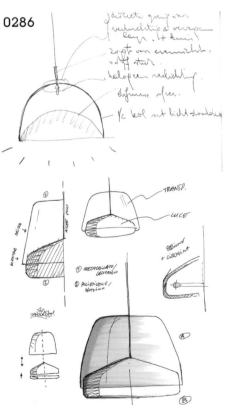

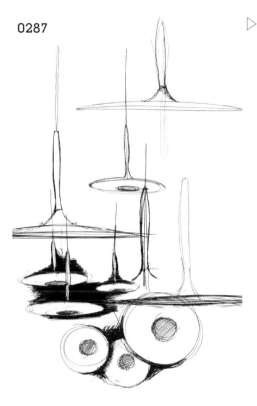

0287

0288

0287 This light fixture belonging to Targetti's Decanter collection, is an exclusive design with a distinctive touch: its sculptural shape. Even when not lit, it serves a decorative element that adds drama to a living or dining room.

0288 To increase the amount of light in a room, consider a cluster of light fixtures, instead of a single one. Manufacturers usually offer sets of ceiling lamps that share the same design and vary in some features, like the color, size and height.

0294 An almost identical tone in the wood of the table, wall and lamp functions to harmonize the dining room space and, together with the white walls, make the accessories — chairs, a bookshelf, a pitcher and some bowls — stand out with their lively colors.

0295 The translucent fabric covering this dining room light emits soft, ethereal lighting, which is incongruent with the the dramatic and irregular peaks, curves and slopes that are created by the underlying metal structure.

0296 Louis Poulsen's Snowball is designed to prevent glare. Its geometry ensures that all the lighting surfaces receive light at an identical angle. It provides uniform lighting above the dining room table, where it is most often used.

0294

0295

0296

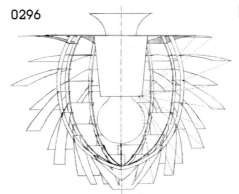

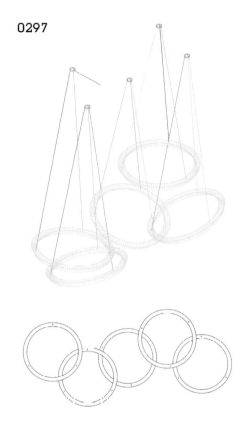

0297 Circular Halo is a hanging lamp with several circular pieces, which create subtle environments, bathed in a magic light. Finished in white lacquer, this lamp was designed by Martín Azúa for Vibia.

0298 Luis Eslava studio designed Agatha, this wood veneer lamp. It is also called "optimist lamp" because of its "petals." Its form provides warmth and a whimsical touch to the dining room.

0299 A methacrylate satin structure covered in a screen of strips can be reinvented in a number of ways; as a suspension lamp, table lamp or two or three leveled standing lamp, because it is modular and stackable. (Bailaora de Metalarte)

0300 This ceiling-mounted lamp designed by Miguel Herranz for LZF stands out for its spectacular organic and dynamic shape. Made of thin wood strips, it provides an interesting interplay of light and shadow.

0299

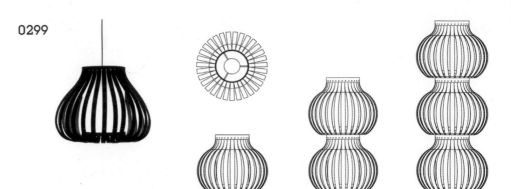

0301

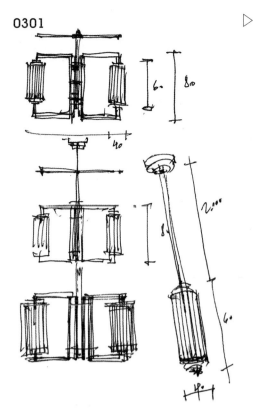

0302

0303

0301 In fifties-sixties style retro living or dining rooms, this hanging lamp design offers a dim, pleasant and comfortable light. This "revival" style is made up of six cylindrical lights distributed symmetrically on a chrome steel base.

0302 The understated but inventive elegance of the Wish lamp from Brazilian designer Fernando Prado for Lumini has become an icon in the lighting design world.

0303 In 2008 Serge Cornelissen designed the LUMO lamp for Steng. It is suspended by two stainless steel cables that allow the adjustment of the height and the tilting angle, and the design lends itself to the use of many of them, depending on the amount of lighting required.

0304 The lighting in this dining room is a study of contrasts. First, there is the combination of an up-lit light box, and two pendulum lights that direct light downward. Within the pendulum lights themselves, there is an opaque inner layer of blown glass inside a perfectly translucent outer layer. The resulting light fixture is unique and remarkable piece.

0305 The fixtures in this room are made of cellular plastic, which means that although it appears solid, the plastic is filled with tiny micropores. This allows the lamp to emit a brighter light, and the geometry of the shape is reflected in the furniture and even in the panes of the windows.

0306 The "Ogle" pendant lamp is a design of the Swedish trio Form Us With Love. The light of the LED bulbs in this dramatic fixture are directable, due to the hidden system in the upper part of the base. The design of this fixture allows it to be used in many variations. It can illuminate a large area as a table light, or a small area as a focus light or spotlight, depending on where the beams of light are aimed. It can also be used as a single unit, or in clusters.

0307

0308

0309

0307 This ceiling light operates under the functional principle of indirect ambient lighting but with a modern structure: the carefree placement of rigid circular plates is reminiscent of the petals of a flower.

0308 Inspired by the silhouettes of trees in a forest, Héctor Serrano designed the lamp, "Woods." The light is surrounded by rectangular pieces of birch suspended irregularly from clear plastic filament. It dims the light and imbues the room with the warm colors of the wood.

0309 The "Campanella" model, designed by Herme Spanish Ciscar and Monica Garcia is made by hand and revolves around the theme of mountaineering. The idea was to transform rough stone into a beautiful object and suspend it from the ceiling with rope and a climbers knot.

0310 This unique and eyecatching LED floor lamp is an up-lighter, but it also radiates a diffuse colored light. The LED are partially enclosed by a matte white body, within which lies a glass diffuser that modulates the colors.

0311 The dim, romantic light of candles is a great option in keeping with the rustic and warm spaces. Traditional and common materials, such as wrought iron, used in a modern way, revitalize this accessory.

0312 Office desk lamps are usually metal, as the material lends itself well to the construction that allows for the precise direction of light. This design uses a warm wood instead and a light shade more suitable for a living room that is also in line with the colors of the furniture.

0313 The musical motif of these lamps add character and whimsy to the warmth of this space, complemented with other details like the support that mimics a melting candle and their unique placement on the frame of the mirror.

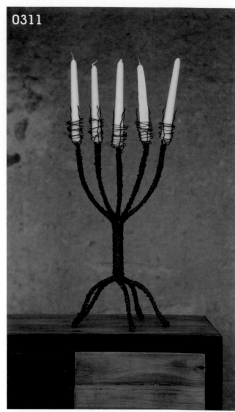

0314

0315

0316

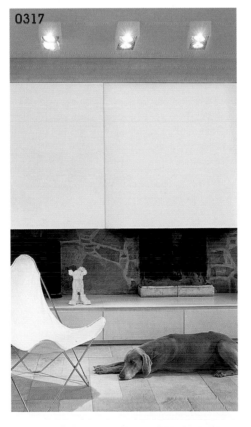

0317

0314 This contemporary design uses directional technology, high-quality materials and agile structures that merge industrial knowledge, with aesthetic delight.

0315 Dynamism and a brilliant metallic quality combine in an ultramodern design that simulates a Mikado game — the traditional wooden stick game with colored points — suspended in the air.

0316 Some areas of this house, like the foyer, the hallways or the L-shaped corners, require special lighting. In this case, a luminous disk in the wall has an impressive presence: its shape and power look like a sun and are in line with the tribal adornments on the shelves.

0317 The "Code" by Trizo21 spotlight allows for an infinite number of configurations. The rounded corners make this light fixture elegant and stylish.

0318 Lamps with jointed structures fulfill an important function as auxiliary lights because they can be directed so that light can reach pointed corners, illuminate specific areas with great precision and direct attention towards decorative details.

0319 "Funiculi" was originally designed in 1979 by Lluis Porqueras. Its pure design and its cable car-like mechanism make this floor lamp a classic for living rooms.

0320 In a space that benefits from a lot of natural light, a standing lamp with a white and generously sized shade favors the ideal distribution of light and has a large reach without being obtrusive.

0319

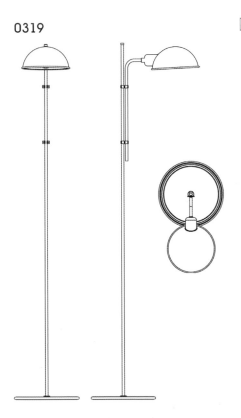

0321

0322

0323

0324

Miquel **Barceló** 1987 1997

RITUALES EN HAITÍ

THE EARTH FROM THE

EGO RIVERA

0321 The distribution of light sources is one of the main aspects to take into account in a living room's interior design. Table lamps that cast light of generous intensity and spread are ideal for lighting corners and crannies that natural light cannot reach.

0322 Clarity is a quality that we associate with good lighting and therefore, table lamps made of transparent and white materials are those with the best functionality. Additionally, these same qualities won't saturate and overwhelm the atmosphere.

0323 Designed by Ferdi Giardini, Nerolia is a table lamp that radiates a diffuse light thanks to the translucent glass, but also diffuses aromatic scents. The beautiful amber cones are made of Murano glass.

0324 The combination of black, red and white creates an impressive contrast that strengthens the shapes of the objects to the maximum. In this case, the table's straight lines and the curious shape of the lamp stand out against the daring red background.

0332 This table's modest technology makes the extendable wings that increase its size almost invisible and they unfold with a single rapid movement. The innovative base attracts a lot of attention and frees all the space under the table to facilitate mobility. (Prora de Bonaldo)

0333 The "Emmei" brand, characterized by designing elegant furniture adapted to contemporary living rooms, has created the Arcanto table. This extendable table has a black-tinted tempered glass top and legs made of extruded aluminum.

0334 Rustic does not necessarily clash with elegance. In this example of the modern trend, that consists of mixing restored or antique tables with contemporary furniture, the table stands out for its characteristic appearance and its practicality.

0335 This table is constructed of an aluminum frame that holds the legs and the glass surface, which is available in greater or lesser opacity. In contrast with the heaviness of wood, a table of this material gives a feeling of lightness and freshness. (Layer de Bonaldo)

0336 In a neutral space it is a good idea to add a touch of color to an unexpected place, like on dining room table legs. Traditional materials, like steel, wood and glass, are combined in an avant-guard style that changes according to the point of view. (Big foot de Bonaldo)

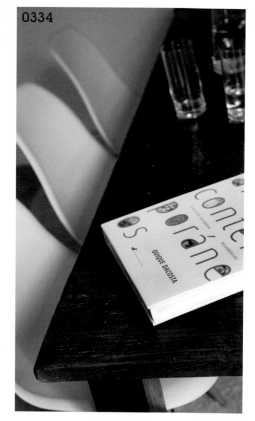

0335

0336

0342 On occasion, it is necessary to add a touch of color to minimalist spaces where white dominates. The table with the transparent orange top gives this living room with a playful character.

0343 This table's design confers a rural and homely style on the dining room because of the gingham pattern on its surface. This pattern, which is typical of a picnic tablecloth, is created by colored stripes that cross perpendicularly to form a square. (Fabian de Kitsuné and e 15)

0344 In addition to its great size, the outward angle of this table's legs, and the base's crossed support beams make it appear forceful, firm and static. However, the functionality of this dining room table can be changed into a desk, for example, with the addition of a powerful floor lamp with great lighting capacity. (Clark de Rodolfo Dordoni for Minotti)

0342

0343

0344

0345

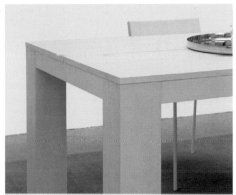

0346

0347

0345 This table designed for e15 follows in the company's tradition of working with natural materials such as wood. Its archetypical shape makes the table a particularly adaptable piece to any living room, and to most diverse lifestyles.

0346 Multiple dining room options are achievable when the table is modular. In addition to the extension that allow it to increase in size, the base position is adjustable. By rotating and folding the parts, they can be combined in myriad different configurations depending on the needs of the occasion. (Isaac de e15)

0347 Wood is the most suitable material for living and dining room tables. Current design tendencies are to highlight, as opposed to mask, the material's texture. In this case, the grain of the wood is left exposed as its own decorative element.

0348 This table's rectangular surface parallels the chromed steel crosspiece in the base, and that, combined with the high quality oak wood it is constructed of, gives the table a sculptural quality. (Dylan de Casamilano).

0349 This table has been constructed of materials that were chosen for their durability under daily use, with a reinforced glass tabletop and varnished aluminum base, and all without sacrificing an elegant and dynamic design. (Diapason de Kreaty Ciacci)

0350 In a predominantly white space, black elements are prominent. In this dining room, the stunning dark oak table is emphasized and only the chair legs stand out dramatically, and cream upholstery almost disappears. (Ettore de Jesse)

0351 A slight, minimalistic dining room table is optimum in smaller spaces. Available in black and platinum white, its curved lines, rounded corners and flat legs are ideal for a futuristic loft. (Slim de Meneghello Paolelli para Kreaty)

0352 The tables designed by Doimo are characterized by the juxtaposition of diverse materials in a harmonious way. Natural wood is paired with polycarbonate; glass is used alongside polyamide. For example, this rectangular table combines curved glass legs with stainless steel tabletop support.

0348

0349

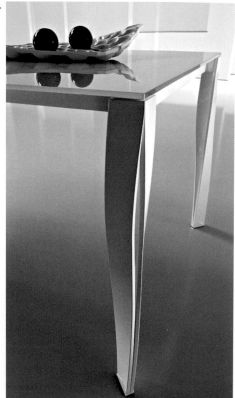

0350

0351

0352

0353 The chairs straight modern lines conform to the ebony table top's linear quality, but they are in dynamic contrast with the ornate table base. In addition to the distinction between the geometric and organic shapes, the dissimiliarty of the materials' textures and sheen — the shine of the ebony, the leather chairs, the lacquered steel, the base's matte wood — is provocative. (Fratino de Bertelé)

0354 For a minimalist environment, stripping a dining room down to its essential requirements can be visually compelling. This simple dining room table has been built with walnut tree wooden beams attached to steel legs. (Anton de e 15)

0355 The "Canaletto" table was designed by Emaf Progetti in 2009. Its substantial construction of solid wood gives it an almost medieval appearance, which complements the ornate chandelier, but is foiled by the contemporary design of the chairs.

0356 Thanks to its durability, flexibility and beauty, wood is the perfect material for the fabrication of tables of all types. These characteristics allow such novel designs as this table's top made of staggered wood boards with their edges cut at 45˚.

0357

0359

0357 This sophisticated and stately dining room is the product of several elements, that impart a sense of lustre. The highly textured deep-pile black area rug is the only piece in the room without shine, and contrasts the hanging light fixture of shiny twisted strips of black glass and the majestic table, whose shiny metallic ornate legs are topped with an ultra-light glass table top. (London de Modà)

0358 Stately tables with moderate curves are striking, especially when finished in a gold lacquer, which enhances their beauty with contemporary textures and high quality materials. (New York de Modà)

0359 The "Orion" table, designed by Ronen Joseph for Pierantonio Bonacina, features a brushed stainless steel structure and a polyethylene top. Its color and finish is similar to that of many of the elements of the room (the steel framed windows, the light glossy floor) allowing the chairs and accent pieces to be the focus.

0360 Glass and wood are two of the most used materials for the construction of furniture. In this example, the contemporary design is exemplified in the warm organic wooden base that is highlighted by the cool glass tabletop.

0361 As the dining room table is usually in the center of the room, why not make it even more overt by choosing one in a bright color and a luminous material? The lively lime color makes the plants and vegetables that are around the dining room's natural green stand out. With a chrome base and clear glass top, the table has an equally commanding presence, that is not minimized by the strong accent colors in the room. (Athene de Modà)

0362

0363

0364

0365

0362 Made of reflective material and with an embellished shape, this oval table is reminiscent of an old fashioned mirror. The organic lines and reflective quality contribute to the polished and refined ambience of the room.

0363 Wenge wood is one the darkest, hardest and most resistant woods in the world. Although it is very difficult to work with, it is ideal for home furniture, especially for pieces that are subject to direct and continuous use like the ones in a dining room. It is so durable, that it is often used for staircases which this table is reminiscent of. (Palermo de Emmemobili)

0364 This table's rounded glass top lets us appreciate the base that has been constructed from hand crafted wooden strips into a braided and curved structure, which doesn't need additional pieces or joints for support. (Nastro de Emmemobili)

0365 Philipp Mainzer designed this table following classical furniture tradition. This table's perfect and balanced proportions make it an outstanding furnishing that irradiates solidity and elegance.

0366

0367

0368

0366 The variety of combinations of materials in the design of dining room tables is limitless. In this example, the chromed steel base, reminiscent of a flower or fountain, is covered in white leather to match the chairs.

0367 This table is remarkable for the sculptural character of the steel legs that endows the space with elegance. The top is made of glass, relieving some of the weight of the base.

0368 Walnut is the most appreciated wood for interior furniture because it can be comfortably worked into small or large boards. The dark grained tone draws beautiful patterns and allows designs, like this table's elliptical base together with chromed metal in the base, to shine. (Sestante de Besana)

0369 An interesting reinterpretation of classical tastes, this arrangement of refined furniture over more risky choices like transparent gauze curtains, a high-pile thread carpet and modern chandelier, still manages to appear cohesive. (Emiliano de Bertelé)

0370 This table's assertive geometry unleashes dynamic movement. The base consists of triangular sides that revolve around the eye of a spiral. A material composed of a base of polyester and acrylic resins loaded with pigmented minerals lends itself well to a design of this kind. (Elica de Zanotta)

0371 The typical support on four-legged support for the dining room table has been replaced by several chromed steel columns arranged like trees in a forest that supports this table's glass tabletop, which can be round or rectangular and is fixed to the steel. (Mille de Donaldo).

0383 The "Ciacci Kreaty Diva Chair" designed by Gino Carollo is an original chair with a dynamic design that calls to mind a racetrack. Made of polycarbonate, the Diva chair is available in various colors.

0384 The "Hans" chair by e15 ensures comfort with its combination of a clean and softly curved wood seat and back. Supported by a thin steel frame these chairs seem to float in the air.

0385 The Wishbone chair is unique among chairs with armrests. Its wonderful design features a wraparound back, which allows for good support. Its design was inspired by classic portraits of Danish merchants seated in Ming Dynasty chairs.

0386 The "Houdini" chair by e15 is an example of quality and precision in woodwork technology, gracefully combining aesthetics with ergonomics.

0387 The "Houdini" chair model offers great versatility. The armchair version features a steam-curved wood back. The chair is available in different finishes: oak or walnut, clear or colored lacquer, and can even be upholstered upon request.

0388 This set of weathered metal chairs contributes to an industrial look. The red finish softens the coldness of the metal while the wood table brings in a warm touch.

0383

0384

0385

0386

0387

0388

0389 People don't normally think of plastic when they're furnishing their homes, but this mindset has begun to change. Plastic furniture can add a modern and cheerful feel to any room of your house, even though plastic furniture is generally used outdoors.

0390 The Sensei Biba chair by Jesse has a minimalist and dynamic aesthetic. Its unique design has a perfectly molded seat, which is ergonomically suited for maximum comfort, which is supported by a chrome-plated frame.

0391 The unusual dull gray distressed finish on this matching table and chair provides a modern and casual accent in a room dominated by white.

0392 Upholstered chairs are a common choice around the dining table. The fabric can match the design of the wallpaper and of the drapes for a uniform décor.

0393 A mixture of materials and styles also has a place in chair design. The "Lolita" chair by Noir-Italy combines upholstery of black leather with chrome legs. The result is an elegant and classically inspired chair.

0394 Plastic is not a noble material. It does, however, allow for the manufacture of products that fit any style, including spaces filled with period furnishings.

0395

0396

0397

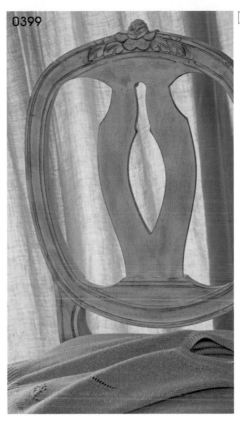

0395 For a compelling twist on classical style, simply keep the bones and use eye-catching fabrics with abstract prints, and high gloss metallic lacquer instead of natural wood. (Remix by Modà)

0396 Chairs, like any other piece of furniture, contribute to defining the style of a room. A wooden chair with simple lines and upholstered seat fits well in a rustic environment.

0397 A classically styled chair acquires a different life when unconventional fabrics are used, and when the wooden parts are finished in aggressive colors. (Dolcevita by Modà)

0398 The choice of chairs depends on the space available and on the room style. Keep in mind that a chair with armrests takes up more space than those without, but they are more comfortable.

0399 The medallion back and the carved wood legs and armrests are characteristic of some antique chairs. This chair finds new life with a new distressed finish and new upholstery that fits in a casual but stylish room.

0400 This is another example of a classical chair design reinterpreted to achieve a contemporary look. The shape is simplified and ornament is limited to a minimum to emphasize form and color.

0401 In this kitchen the doors, cabinets and drawers have a glossy, lacquered finish. They act as the main decorative element in the room and create a minimalist, contemporary and elegant atmosphere.

0402 A simple sideboard can be quite versatile. Its surface can serve as a table, while its shelves allow glassware to be displayed and ready for use. In this kitchen, glasses and wicker baskets are artfully presented on the lower shelves of a sideboard.

0403 A glass cabinet like this not only stores kitchen products, it also gives them added character. These bottles, protected and emphasized by the glass, become the room's prominent decorative element.

0404 Open shelves near a kitchen island are certainly convenient. Shallow shelves are great to display jars of herbs and spices. They can be nice to look at and you can quickly spot the one you need!

0405 The easiest way to create a sparse and minimalist kitchen is to opt for white cabinetry with colorful accent pieces. These bursts of color will pop in a white kitchen, adding contrast and interest to the room.

0406 This kitchen shows how the concepts of symmetry and asymmetry can be played with in order to organize storage units. The parallelism between the cooking surfaces on both sides of the stove is complemented by the diminutive, wall-mounted shelving unit.

0407 Along with basic cooking utensils, you can also display potted plants on your kitchen shelves. Not only do they give color and life to the room, they will also help absorb any unfavorable smells. And don't forget the clock, essential for checking cooking times and a key element in any kitchen.

0408 This Tecnocucina design is based in symmetry. The cabinets, arranged symmetrically around the sink, are reflected in the glossy floor and give off a surreal and modern feel.

0401

0402

0403

0404

0405

0406

0407

0408

0409 Who said that the kitchen is only for cooking and eating? The intimate and comfortable atmosphere of this room makes it the ideal place to read, study and relax. This inviting environment was created by adding some books and artwork among the jars of spices.

0410 Labeling drawers by their contents shows how organization and decoration can go hand in hand. This simple detail, together with the rounded shape and the pale tone of the drawers, provide the kitchen with a daring and futuristic character.

0411 The orange cabinetry in this monochromatic kitchen has great visual impact. The color of the cabinets is echoed throughout the accent pieces, such as the hanging oven mitts.

0412 These wooden shelves store many decorative items as well as dishes that see daily use. The plates, teacups and glasses that sprinkle the shelves make the kitchen an inviting and homey space in which one can feel at ease.

0409

0410

0411

0412

0413

0414

0415

0417

0416

0413 If there is an element that defines this kitchen, it is its shine. The cabinets, the steel surfaces and the floor all are highly reflective. The combination of materials and colors enhances the sensation of coldness and purity.

0414 Using a curtain instead of a cabinet door is an economical and original solution. It can also be used in addition to a cupboard door, if you wish to display the door only at select times. Furthermore, this added touch brings color to a room and harmonizes with other fabrics that are present, like window curtains or tea towels.

0415 If you dream of a really elegant and chic kitchen, overcome your fear of the color black. A trick for not overwhelming the room with darkness is to keep the main elements (for example the cabinets) black, and leave small details in lighter colors to create an effective contrast.

0416 In a kitchen's design, storage units can play a central role if their bold color predominates throughout the room. This kitchen's blue tone exudes liveliness and serenity, combining perfectly with the wood and stainless steel.

0417 Equipped with sophisticated gliding mechanisms, these drawers allow for optimal accessibility and feature refined details. Their chestnut wood harmonizes with the black countertop.

0418 This L-shaped countertop provides a great additional storage space and, at the same time, offers a surface that can function as a countertop on which to cook and eat and, why not, as a work and study area as well.

0419 These space-efficient cabinets create a modern and distinct atmosphere. Installing only one wall of cabinets allows you to have a more minimalist kitchen and, on the other hand, the colors and lines become the main decorative element in the room.

0420 In this case it is the cabinets that stand out in the kitchen environment. In contrast with the black-and-white striped walls, their solid color and glossy finish draws attention.

0421 This drawer, belonging to the Casale model by Rational, has wooden separators that prevent the plates from moving. Smoked oak wood is the perfect choice for giving character to a kitchen and creating a modern country home atmosphere.

0422 The storage modules in this kitchen are distributed in a "U" shape, acting as the kitchen's work surfaces. In an open space, this structure creates the feeling of seclusion that the walls do not bring and separates the cooking area from the rest of the room.

0423 Tecnocucina architects design spacious and open kitchens that are connected to the living room. Under the premise of uniting functionality and innovation with design and aesthetics, they have converted this space into a modern, elegant and exciting sanctuary.

0424 Behind these pocket doors designed by Armani, everything but the fridge and freezer are hidden. With bronze paneling and a plaited texture, these doors create a sober and linear style that is extremely sophisticated.

0422

0423

0424

0425 In this space tones of black and white predominate, with the exception of the lone wooden countertop. The scale's most intense color is found in the cabinet with the chrome base.

0426 At times a simple feature, such as this unique handle, is capable of turning a piece of furniture into one of the room's defining elements. Achieving an original kitchen can be as easy as looking after small details and finishes.

0427 Laminate, which has always been perceived as a high-quality, resistant and superior product, has been reinvented by Tecnocucina in the Graphos model. This kitchen is aimed at a consumer with refined taste in search of style and rigor.

0428 Designed as part of an affordable architecture project, G.One cabinets don't have visible handles and their lightly rounded corners soften the set's effect. Its style is reminiscent of the 1950s and 1960s, yet it is compatible with smartphones.

0425

0426

0428

0427

0429 It is always easier to have an organized kitchen, in which the exact whereabouts of each pan and dish are known. Even though their exterior is simple, the inside of these cabinets is compartmentalized so that each item occupies its own place.

0430 Cutting-edge appliances, adjoined at the center of the wall, are completely surrounded by kitchen cabinets. This wall unit adds to the elegant contrast of black and steel, giving the kitchen a museum feel.

0431 In a small kitchen, look for ways to take advantage of all available space. This drawer is a good example – despite being situated in a corner, its diagonal opening mechanism allows you to gain storage space.

0437 The outward simplicity of this kitchen does not extend into the interior of its cabinetry. At first perceived as a sparse and minimalist space, upon opening any cabinet one finds the true character of this room.

0438 Inspired by the architecture of Giuseppe Terragni, the design of this unit pays utmost attention to detail. Dividers allow every type of cutlery and kitchen utensil to occupy its own place, creating a design that is both practical and sleek.

0439 For the Dada brand, the kitchen is the heart of the house. Given this, a kitchen must not only reflect our personal style, it must fuse design with functionality. In this kitchen two qualities stand out: organization and rationality.

0440 Designed by Dante Bonuccelli, in this kitchen each utensil has its own place. It is a perfect example of how multiple forms of storage can be combined in a single space, such as shelves of various sizes, cabinets and compartmentalized units.

0437

0438

0439

0440

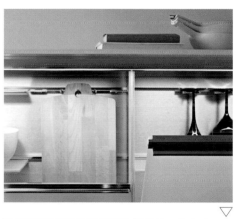

0446

0447

0448

0449

0450

0451

0446 Mobalco's Organica is a design that is both environmentally friendly and constructed with superior-quality materials. The distribution of its appliances across a wide kitchen creates distinct areas and allows for multiple users to perform tasks simultaneously.

0447 Wall-mounted cabinets with doors that open vertically are both sensible and stylish. They maximize your storage space above the counter and add a subtle, modern touch to the room's design.

0448 Would you like to be able to hide or display the contents of your kitchen cabinets according to the occasion? This system of adjustable shelf coverings allows both options. The contents become more decorative when the cover is lowered and they are on display; lifting the cover, on the other hand, conveniently conceals the contents.

0449 In order to create a more refined, elegant and minimalist kitchen, it helps not to have superfluous items in view. Installing a compartment like this can help to keep utensils in an orderly manner and achieve a zen kitchen.

0450 If your kitchen is small, it is not impossible to create a minimalist atmosphere. Choosing appliances on a smaller scale allows you to save space, and well-ordered cabinets can do wonders for maximizing limited storage space.

0451 These American walnut doors hide more than they seem. To take advantage of a corner space, a swiveling cabinet has been installed that illustrates Charles Eames' phrase, who this kitchen is inspired by: "The details are not details. The details are the design,"

0452 This island is made up of two areas differentiated by function: the cooking area, crowned by the range hood, and the countertop, which is both a food preparation surface and bar. A pale gray tone extends the length of the island, visually uniting the two areas.

0453 A simple way to create a breakfast bar is to place a raised countertop with a pair of stools on one end of an island. This elevated surface is ideal for quick meals and transitions the kitchen into the dining room.

0454 Although this island is diminutive and its functions may seem limited, one end can easily be set up as a breakfast bar. In small kitchens, islands help to make the most of all available space and can also offer an improvised office when we need it.

0455 One way to enhance the functionality of an island is to integrate kitchen appliances into it. It is likely that gas and electricity will need to be installed, so it is wise to rely on the help of a professional.

0452

0453

0454

0455

0456 In a spacious kitchen, a large island can be divided into working areas (sink, cooking surface and countertop, for example) to allow various people to use it at the same time. In this way, the island is converted into an accessible and comfortable place in which to gather and prepare meals.

0457 This model by G.One is functional and formal in its simpicity. The island's shape, a Schiffini design, creates an uninterrupted surface that widens in order to accommodate a small dining area.

0458 An island is just a piece of furniture in the middle of a kitchen, but given its versatility, it is one of the kitchen's most used spaces. This island illustrates how we can take full advantage of this piece of furniture by adding compartments, working areas and a good countertop on which to enjoy food.

0456

0457

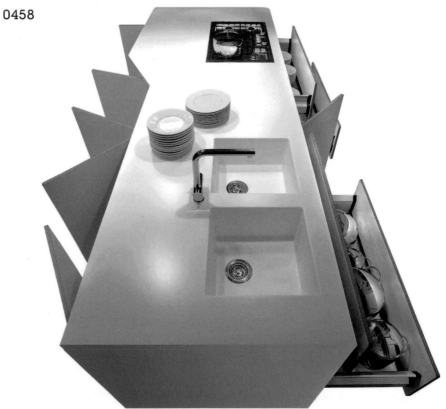

0458

0459 The kitchen island does not necessarily have to match the rest of the kitchen's cabinetry. It is a focal point in its own right and so it makes perfect sense to have an island that stands out in shape, color and surface material.

0460 Why not convert an island into the kitchen's center of attention? Instead of coating it with light colors to reduce its visual weight, we can use dark and heavy materials so that it stands out. Covered with supplies of different shapes and colors, it becomes an extraordinary storage piece.

0461 Positioned between the open kitchen and the dining room, this tall table can also function as an island. Accompanied by three pairs of stools, it is a place to gather for a meal. Used as a surface for storing kitchenware or for preparing meals, however, it is a functional and elegant island.

0462 The Vivo chimney, from the MCZ Brand, enhances the rustic yet sophisticated mood created by this dark island. Its glossy surface reflects the flames from the fireplace, providing a much-needed refuge from the chaos of daily life.

0463

0464

0465

0466

0467

0468

0463 Even though this is a kitchen, the island has a distinct office or dining room table feel to it. This elegant piece of furniture transforms the room's atmosphere and gives it a new meaning. It is certainly the most dominant feature in the room.

0464 The generous size of this Aero island, by Mobalco, is supported by small, metal legs. As its name indicates, it almost appears to float. Rosewood is used in both the island and the cabinet doors, unifying the overall space and giving it elegance.

0465 To get the most out of an island, drawers, shelves and cabinets can be installed. In this way, you gain storage space and you have everything necessary for eating and cooking together in the same space.

0466 This L-shaped countertop is made up of different units and levels that help divide the space according to function. The modern lighting, sink fixtures and accessories complete the look of this sleek and minimalist kitchen.

0467 An island's countertop must be suitable for a variety of uses, so it helps if its surface is durable. In this case, however, a more aesthetic than functional style has been chosen: although the wood is delicate, it gives the island a modern and timeless touch.

0468 These two intersecting islands are made of different materials: Calacatta marble and wood. When combined, the islands provide four very different areas: the food preparation area, the cooking area, the dining area and a multipurpose surface.

0469

0470

0471

0472

0473

CHOICE BLEND
TUDOR
TEA
Earl Grey
Net. Weight 8 oz 227g
Especially blended for and imported by
Ferd. Andersen & CO. Established 1885

0469 It is not difficult to create a welcoming and intimate atmosphere, in which you can sit and enjoy a coffee while you read the newspaper. The combination of the Dandy table and the Party stools, designed by O&G, creates this retreat in the middle of any house.

0470 You can create a breakfast area by mounting a bar against the wall and adding a pair of barstools. The optimum depth of a bar is 18 inches (45 cm), and its height oscillates between 35 and 41 inches (90-105 cm). The length will depend on the space available: at 59 inches (1.5 m), two adults can fit comfortably.

0471 The O&G Ping Pong console table can be placed in any corner of the house to create an intimate and versatile atmosphere. Discrete and functional, it creates the perfect place both to work and to share an informal meal. You can combine the table with Relax foldable chairs, designed by O&G.

0472 If you have an island available, you can use one of its ends as a breakfast bar. Some placemats and barstools are all that you need to turn one section of the island into a dining space.

0473 Removed from the clamor of the kitchen, this table placed by a hallway wall offers a calm refuge in a space we would not expect to find one. It also demonstrates that, when referring to what is known as a "breakfast bar," bigger does not necessarily mean better.

0474 In this house, the dining room is found in the kitchen. A small wooden table and a pair of chairs located in one end of the room are a practical solution for making the absolute most of the kitchen space and having at hand everything necessary to set the table.

0475 If you have a kitchen that opens into a dining room, one option is to place a table between the two spaces. Small and discrete, this table is in harmony with the other furnishings in the room and effectively separates the two spaces.

0474

0475

0476 The Bridge kitchen countertop by Armani/Dada has grey oak finishes, and stainless steel and water-proof technical fabric covered with glass plaques that emphasize the room's minimalist and functional design.

0477 To counteract the birchwood's warm finish, a very thin white acid glass countertop can be set up. Although the thick surfaces transmit modernity, thin countertops are more economical.

0478 Black and white are at opposite ends of the color spectrum but work very well together. This contrast of colors gives the kitchen elegance. The space's central piece, the countertop, is in grey, the palette's intermediate color.

0479 Wooden countertops are beautiful and natural, but the porous nature of wood is problematic; it is a delicate material, easily stained and scratched. The coutertops are available in a wide range of colors and can offer a modern or rustic appearance.

0480 Stainless steel countertops, frequently used in restaurants, are resistant to acids and heat and are very hygienic. They are ideal for giving a modern, functional atmosphere to a kitchen; the only inconvenience is their high price.

0476

0477

0478

0479

0480

0481

0482

0483

0484

0481 The rustic atmosphere of this kitchen is provided by the wood and stone walls and floors. The countertop in stainless steel balances the effect by providing space and functionality. Stainless steel is easy to clean but scratches easily.

0482 This office design displays an interesting idea: two storage areas sunk into the countertop so that spices and dressings can always be available.

0483 Porphyry is a resistant non-slippery material, long-lasting and cheap to maintain. Beautiful, elegant and sober, this brushed brown porphyry countertop is 3 inches (8 cm) thick and matches perfectly with César Yara's personality (the designer of this kitchen).

0484 This is a Laminam ceramic slate countertop. Thin and light, it is only 0.3 inches (7 mm) thick and is created by layering fiberglass between two 0.1-inch (3 mm) sheets of slate. Its dark and somewhat dull color contrasts well with the cupboards' vibrant red.

0485 In a small space like this, the countertop can double as a breakfast bar. Remember that the depth must be a minimum of 12 inches (30 cm) to be comfortable for users. If the ceiling is high enough, you can place a shelf above the space in order to provide more storage.

0486 A food hatch with a pocket door prevents food smells from wafting into the dining room. By closing the door, you can also define two separate spaces.

0487 Exactly the same color as the kitchen and living room, this hatch connects both spaces visually and lets light and air circulate. Furthermore, the plant and mirror placed at both ends of the food hatch turn it into the heart of the room.

0488 Installing a food hatch can be as simple as placing a piece of furniture in front of a door. It also allows for strategic placement of dishes when serving food.

0489 In this kitchen, the wall opening is decorative rather than practial: the kitchen is presented as a picture, framed by the opening. And the shelf is a convenient place to add small details that give a touch of color to a room in which white dominates.

0490

0491

0493

0492

0494

0490 An extractor hood is an important electrical appliance since it eliminates smoke, smells and heat produced when cooking. For a glass-ceramic hob it is recommended that hoods are placed 22 inches (55 cm) from the cooktop, covering the area completely.

0491 An elegant wine chiller is found in the Bridge kitchen. It is closed by a plaited textured glass pocket door with borders and anodized aluminum handles. The inside, like the structure, has sucupira wood laminates.

0492 Having a TV monitor in the kitchen can be handy; you can prepare a meal while following the instructions from your favorite cooking show! A ceiling-mounted TV screen is practical since it does not take up valuable counter space.

0493 Stainless steel appliances are a popular choice and can be paired with any color scheme. Bold or dark colors are not a problem since stainless steel reflects light.

0494 A built-in microwave and oven on the wall offers advantages: it saves space and lets you keep the kitchen tidier; it makes a feauture of the electrical appliances and draws attention to their decorative appeal.

0495 A shiny stainless steel suspended hood, from the Elica brand, reveals vibrant color on the inside surface: available in turquoise and red, this splash of color contrasts stunningly with the neutrally colored kitchen.

0496 Range hoods don't have to be utilitarian kitchen devices that blend into the background. Elica's Platinum model is a sleek stainless steel model that reflects the design of the cooktop below; together they become the center of this kitchen design.

0497 Elica's Wave model, made of stainless steel, includes halogen atmosphere lighting. It not only lights up the working area but also illuminates the surrounding area.

0498 Compartmentalizing the island helps to organize the working areas: the sink has been separated from the range with a glass panel that gives this area a ping-pong table appearance.

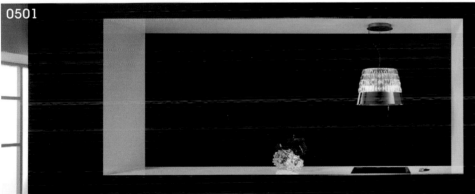

0499 Stainless steel is the favorite material for manufacturing design hoods. It gives an aura of modernity to the kitchen and is highly resistant to corrosion, but it is easily stained with fingerprints and can scratch easily. Therefore, it helps to choose a hood with an anti-scratch system.

0500 This stainless steel and glass wall hood is an elegant example of Cube lighting. Enveloped by the opaque-toned glass, the light gives the kitchen a surreal halo. This Elica design is clean, delicate and ethereal.

0501 Made of stainless steel and glass, this Victoria model gives off sparkles of light that refract and divide into colors. More like a lamp than a hood, it is a technological jewel that inspires our day-to-day life and transcends the principle of mere utility.

0502 Vogue Black Leather combines functionality with the beauty of exclusive materials: stainless steel and black leather. The model, which looks like an architectural piece in miniature, has a particulary high-suction capacity, especially suitable for large kitchens.

0503 Suspended above the kitchen's peninsula, Grace is a white glass and stainless steel hood designed by Elica. The white echoes the peninsula's countertop and contrasts with the vertical surfaces' dark tones.

0504 Elica's Space model is fitted out with the EDS3 system, which allows it to work so silently that it cannot be heard at low speeds. It represents an over 35% reduction to acoustic pollution compared to traditional hoods, and it doesn't reduce the suction capacity.

0505 This hood's height and shape allow an uncommon usage: it takes advantage of the surface as one more storage area. This electric device is suspended as a swing above the kitchen island and offers us more space.

0506 Designed for Elica by David Lewis, the Bogart model presents pure geometric shapes for light to play on. The inclined surface that crosses over the glass hood is the highlight of this special accessory.

0507 The Stone Gallery hood is equipped with LED technology, guaranteeing ideal lighting for the cooking area. Extremely ecological, the LEDs last up to ten times longer than traditional lamps and allows up to 90% savings on electrical energy.

0508 Despite the advantages of glass ceramic hob and induction plates, traditional kitchen lovers still prefer gas. Having the ranges in line is a very practical solution that allows you to cook several dishes at a time.

0509 More than a hood, Elica's Legend model looks like a sculpture suspended in the air. It includes a perimeter suction system and five halogen bulbs. Available in shining stainless steel and glass, this revolutionary circle is absolutely eye-catching.

0504

0505

0506

0507

0508

0509

0510

0511

0512

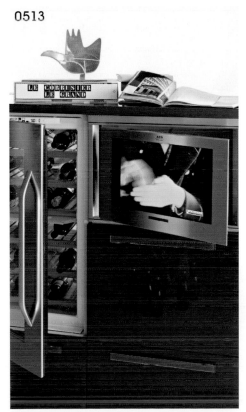

0513

0514

0510 Kora, designed by Tecnocucina, is a kitchen with oak finishes. The electrical devices are disguised by the wood. The cooking and oven areas have the darkest tones, standing out visually and telling us about the inhabitants' tastes.

0511 The Nuvola kitchen, by Dada, presents original electrical devices: a wine cooler, an oven and a fridge with a quick freeze option and refrigerate function. All made with stainless steel, they take advantage of the island's smaller space.

0512 Designed by César Yara, this sink can be hidden beneath the sliding glass white acid countertops. Upon closing, these are fused with the peninsula's countertop, made of the same material, widening the kitchen's working area.

0513 Screens are a ubiquitous part of our lives and this invasion is also reflected in the kitchen. With technological advances, it is possible to set up a television screen on a cupboard door or a microwave door.

0514 In order to choose a fridge and freezer, we have to take into account how many people live in the house. If it is a large family, it is helpful to have these functions separated. If you are looking for a non-conventional kitchen, an option is to hide them in one of the kitchen cupboards.

0515 The taps set up on the wall offer a solution for those sinks that don't include a place to install the taps. This old-fashioned polished brass tap gives the room a retro touch and suits the rural kitchen atmosphere.

0516 If it is a double sink, it is important to set up a revolving tap which rotates 180° and aims the water towards both sinks. This double handle tap model has also got buttons for opening and closing the water flow.

0517 An ecological solution that single-handle taps offer nowadays is called "always open cold." We tend to leave the handle in a central position, which represents a waste of energy; with this solution only cold water comes out when we open the tap.

0518 In a very personal environment, it is worth considering choosing a tap that has a design matching the room's style. It is best not to think about the tap individually but consider it in relation to the rest of the kitchen design.

0519 Removable taps allow the water stream range to increase, and are ideal for washing vegetables, rinsing dinner surfaces, washing the sink or reaching any difficult-to-access area. After using them, we only have to put them back in their original position.

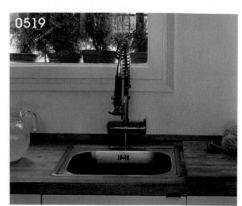

0520

0521

0522

0523

0520 Given the mixing taps' ease of opening, they can almost always be opened to the limit. To avoid this waste of water, a mechanism has been invented to open it in two phases, with an intermediate limit that offers enough flow for habitual uses, which reduces water consumption by 50%.

0521 Given the wide range of kitchen taps available, it is best to consider the way the kitchen will be used. If you cook a lot, install a high pipe tap which is handy for filling large pots and pans.

0522 The stainless steel sink and tap represent an elegant contrast to this butter-colored silk-lacquered kitchen designed by César Yara. The geometrical shapes of the tap enhance the space's tidy and functional nature.

0523 Due to their simplicity and aesthetic appeal, single-handle taps are more and more common. They offer an advantage that we have to consider with regard to double-handle taps: they are a lot more efficient and conserve water.

0531 Bold colors add energy to any room, including kitchens. Kitchens used to be functional spaces as opposed to living rooms which were for socializing. As the line between these uses blurs, colors become more important, making the kitchen more inviting.

0532 If you want to give your kitchen a bar atmosphere, you can paint one of the walls black and fill it with signs and writing related to the space. With this simple idea, the place acquires a livelier character.

0533

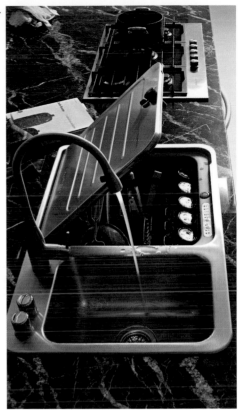

0534

0533 This Nuvola kitchen, designed by Luca Meda for Dada, presents an attractive contrast between the cupboard's brilliant white lacquer, the Grigio Carnico marble of the countertops (1.5-inch/4 cm thick) and the sink, electrical appliances and handles' stainless steel.

0534 If you have a kitchen with natural light, stainless steel is a good choice of material for the countertops. It reflects the light and gives off a sparkling and smooth texture. In addition, these qualities make it perfect for a minimalist atmosphere.

0535

0536

0537

0538

0539

0540

0535 Wood is grained, natural and warm, the opposite of lacquer's smooth, artificial and cold appearance. This kitchen highlights the contrasts and emphasizes the human activities that take place in this room.

0536 The Rational brand's Atmos kitchen is made of cherry tree melamine. This material presents a wide variety of colors and textures; it is resistant and prevents the spread of microorganisms, so it is ideal for aseptic environments.

0537 Mixing materials and textures is not easy, but can provide a colorful and sensitive richness to an environment. The mixture of pale tones enhances light and visual width and gives the space intimate warmth.

0538 The shining lacquered finish gives the kitchen a modern, technological and sophisticated look. In this space, the combination of white and black creates an elegant contrast. To counteract the lacquer's smoothness, you may want to introduce some wooden surfaces, adding a warmth that a purely laquered finish does not have.

0539 In this piece colors and textures are mixed. The fold-out counter's sucupira wood combines with the base and handle's bronze color. In contrast with the wood's grained texture and smooth base, the foldable door displays a plaited texture.

0540 Designed by César Yara, this kitchen shines thanks to the brushed finish that has been given to the countertop and back wall's stainless steel. To achieve this finish they use soft abrasives, which create a reflective and shining effect over the metal.

0541 In this room's lighting, the lighting structure itself is what stands out. A spider ceiling lamp hangs over the central surface and spotlights emerge as though they were its legs, claiming the spotlight as the main decorative objective in the room.

0542 The central table area has to be a welcoming communal center, and light helps to define this atmosphere. The most appropriate type of lighting for this effect is a hanging or ceiling lamp that focuses on the table and creates a halo of intimacy around it.

0543 This kitchen island is lit up by two light bulbs that direct light towards the objects found below and project shadows onto the floor. You have to make sure that the shadows do not fall directly on the work surfaces because they could interfere with the activities taking place on the island.

0544 In this kitchen, a combination of fitted lamps or bull's eyes provides the ambient or general lighting. Strung along the ceiling they feature an exterior wall lamp that controls the light and directs it towards different points in the room.

0545 In the kitchen's working areas we need detailed lighting which gives enough light to enable food preparation. These adjustable wall lamps project light downwards and project sufficient lighting onto the countertop and board.

0546 When placing a ceiling lamp, it is very important to calculate the height at which it is located in order to avoid obstructing sightlines between the diners. Practical and versatile, the adjustable height hanging lamps offer a solution to this problem.

0547 The lighting that this wall lamp produces is mostly decorative: its function is aesthetic rather than practical. Since this is not a working area, it is an appropriate light for emphasizing select details; in the case of this kitchen, it is a plate that we particularly like.

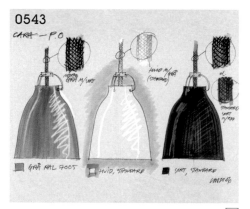

0545

0546

0547

0548

0549

0550

0551

0552

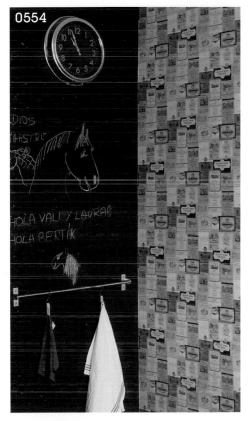

0554

0556

0553

0555

0548 It is not only the choice and arrangement of furniture that matters in a kitchen design: the practical nature of the electrical appliances needs to be considered, and the utensils should be carefully chosen since they are often left in sight and capture attention more than countertops and cupboards.

0549 It is not difficult to give a kitchen a vintage look. It is often enough to choose a functional object that has some outstanding feature. In this case, it is a set of antique weigh scales that gives the room a retro focus.

0550 A drawer is not the only storage place for cutlery. Zinc buckets represent an original way of storing it in plain sight. This detail shows how changing up what we are accustomed to can become a decorative idea.

0551 The candles form part of the decorative lighting so, more than a source of light, they are used for aesthetic value. The three lively colored and hindu-inspired lanterns that we find in the thin shelf above the sink give the kitchen an oriental atmosphere.

0552 This wine lover's kitchen shows how the combination of elements can be played with to create a unique and harmonious atmosphere that reflects personal tastes. The wine labels combine beautifully with the tea towels.

0553 In this kitchen details are paramount: the hanger, the tablemat, the wicker drawer, the glass jar for the rice. Ultimately it is the small details that convert a room into a personal space and tell us about the people that live there.

0554 The kitchen is an ideal place in which to install a slate wall. Amusing and useful at the same time, both children and adults can enjoy its whimsy. It can be used for drawing, writing inspiring verses or noting the most prosaic shopping list.

0555 What hanger can be more appropriate for the kitchen than one in which the hooks are the cutlery? It may be a small thing, but it's a detail that helps to define the room's essence and highlight the kitchen's identity.

0556 This kitchen sink is organized in a rational way: the sliding door surfaces allow for draining, storing vegetables and food preparation. It is an example of how small details can unite aesthetics and functionality.

0557 When designing a custom headboard, you can make the most of it by creating alcoves in both sides of the bed and using hollows as decorative shelves. In this room, the headboard and plaster alcoves fuse with the wall, emanating calm because of their uniform white treatment.

0558 A headboard can combine the greatest elegance with maximum versatility. This beautiful piece of wooden furniture, with its cloth stripes that match the cushions, also acts as a headrest and a ledge for functional and decorative objects.

0559 A floor to ceiling curtain made of heavy fabric serves as a divider between the walk-in closet and the bed. Although not a headboard per se, it does mark the head of the bed aesthetically.

0560 A white line extends from the bed's structure and marks out a section of the wall to suggest a headboard. This technique is at once non-traditional and incredibly chic.

0561 Designed by Gino Carollo, the Giotto bed is based on a single line that extends upward to form the headboard. The surface is suspended upon a circular base, which can be fixed or rotating. This aerodynamic and imaginative design bestows a sort of New York atmosphere upon the room.

0562 If you choose a bed whose structure already includes the headboard, make sure that the combination follows the same decorative line as the surroundings. Smooth and dynamic, these rounded shapes look good in any environment.

0563 An original way to tackle the installation of a bed's headboard is with a concrete wall, like this half-height wall with a distinct finish to that of the actual wall, whose ledge is also used as a bedside table.

0564 If you do not have enough space available for placing bedside tables, you can set up a narrow one-piece headboard, made of chipboard or MDF, with a niche on each side that functions as a shelf.

0561

0562

0563

0564

0565 Configured upon rails, the bunk beds, bedside table and small stack of shelves enjoy maximum mobility and give the bedroom a wide possibility of combinations. Also, the rails allow you to stack the beds during the day and optimize room space.

0566 In smaller spaces, using furniture on wheels helps to make the maximum use of available space. In a wide room like this one, the arrangement of the pieces can be changed up at will to accomodate the distinct purposes the room serves at different times throughout the day.

0567 The headboard is not only a practical, essential element of bedroom design, rather it can also serve as the main decorative piece. Consider the atmosphere you want to create and choose one that helps you to transmit it. Installing some matching bedside tables may also enhance the chosen atmosphere.

0568 A simple and sober dark wooden structure constitutes a functional and sophisticated headboard. This material, of elegant and traditional appearance, combines with any type of decoration and does not require great maintenance.

0565

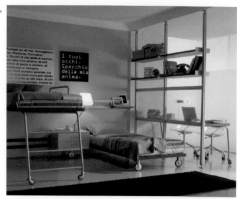

0566

0567

0568

0569

0570

0571

0572

0569 This bedroom plays with the combination of friezes in multiple forms. The wall, made of decorative tiles, plays with the bedspread, and the wooden headboard draws another frieze on the ceramic wall with its shape. This jumbled design gives the room a rococo look.

0570 If the bedroom wall is an incredible design feature unto itself, if it has some qualities that give the space personality, it is not necessary to attach a headboard. Simply allow the wall to convey its full impact.

0571 This smooth, spongy quilted headboard seems to invite you to dream. The depth of the dark blue color and blandness of its texture conveys ultimate relaxation.

0572 Even though headboards serve a functional purpose (protecting the head and maintaining the bedclothes in place), often they have a purely decorative role. An original and easy way to create a headboard is to install a curtain bar and hang cushions on it.

0573 Some bedrooms benefit from a very utilitarian, simple approach to headboard design, such as this plain white rectangle configuration.

0574 In small bedrooms, the headboard's thickness can pose a problem. Consider sourcing and sizing a section of thin wood that will give a classy and warm touch, without having to take up much space.

0575 A practical solution for resolving the headboard issue is to place a lengthy cushion against a wooden rail. The cushion cover can be switched seasonally or whenever a new look is desired.

0576 If you want to give a cheerful and youthful appearance to a bedroom, decorate the headboard in a playful pattern. A practical solution is to place adhesive vinyls, but you can also choose a ready-patterned headboard.

0577 A neutral colored upholstered headboard goes very well with the other furniture and, more importantly, with any style. It is not only the perfect choice if you want to create a classic atmosphere with a distinguished mark, but also for obtaining a chic and sophisticated atmosphere.

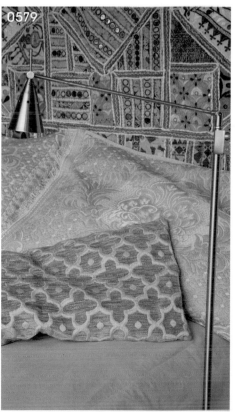

0579

0580

0578 Developed by Cia International in collaboration with the designer Giuseppe Viganò, this bed displays a headboard formed by three colored stripes that match the bedclothes. A vivid colored headrest will transmit energy and dynamism, and is ideal for a children's bedroom.

0579 If you want to crown your bed with a headboard but you do not have many resources available, a practical and cheap solution is to place a tapestry on the wall. An oriental-style patchwork, for example, will give life and color to the atmosphere and will fill you with energy when you get up.

0580 Installed in one of the rooms of the prestigious Hilton Athens, this COCO-MAT bed has an innovative ergonomic base. Hand-made and constructed of beech wood slats and rubber strips, it offers an isometric support, maximum elasticity and perfect ventilation.

0581 Even though it is more conventional, there is no need to place the bed's headboard in contact with a wall. A bed placed in the center of the room leaves the walls free for elements such as stacks of shelves, helping to optimize the space and bringing a surprising and inspiring touch to the bedroom.

0582 Headboard design today is trending toward taller and taller, but consider a modest, proportional look such as in this space.

0583 In cases where the bed is placed against a feature wall clad in vibrant wallpaper, consider forgoing an actual headboard.

0584 Instead of one headboard, it seems that there are three. The bed's structure, elevated upon the wall, stands out above the wooden headboard, which is framed by the white wall in turn. This triple set of textures and contrasts gives the room a Russian doll effect.

0585

0586

0587

0585 In order to create a minimalist atmosphere, opt for a simple headboard: light, thin, white and, if possible, of low height. Sometimes the simplest bedroom is the ideal one.

0586 To create an appropriate resting atmosphere, it is helpful to use natural materials (especially for the bed and headboard) and to situate electronic devices away from the bed.

0587 If you have a house with an attic, what could be better than using it as a bedroom? In this case, consider placing the bed backing on to the rest of the house and build a small wall that separates the two spaces. The same medium height wall will function as a headboard.

0588 Various theories exist about which direction the bed should face in order to facilitate rest. Here, the bed is situated between the window and the mirror, to make best use of natural light.

0589 This colonial style bed is a Bertelé design. Constructed of ebony and forged iron (used in the columns and the canopy), this piece recalls the elegance of the colonial era and becomes the focal point of the room.

0590 In the case of building a concrete headboard or taking advantage of a master beam as a headrest, there is no reason to limit it to covering the width of the bed; it can extend along the entire wall. In this way, a feeling of dynamism and functionality is obtained.

0591 Honey, designed by Arik Levy, is a bed composed of one thin line, upholstered with fabric or with leather. For the designer, the challenge was to create a bed of minimal design, conformable to different spaces, easy to install and of simple, modern and elegant proportions.

0592

0593

0594

0595

0596

0592 That which during the day appears to be just one of the room's many wardrobes reveals itself to be the bed when night falls. Foldable beds are very practical in bedrooms that double as office or study space.

0593 Choose a simple, utilitarian headboard such as this plain white shelf when a busy, eclectic approach is taken with the rest of the bedroom decoration.

0594 Some bedrooms are only large enough to fit a small bed and a tiny bedside table adjacent. An idea for making the most use of the area below the bed is to place some hidden boxes under the structure.

0595 Installing the bed below the window is an ideal decision for a room completely dedicated to rest. In this way, the morning light lets you read in bed without having to get up. By night, a lovely fireplace provides the heat and lighting that by day is provided by the window.

0596 Designed by Stefano Gallizioli, the Elyseo Classic bed structure is upholstered with a removable fabric cover. The sumptuous texture and curved lines create a welcoming atmosphere in the bedroom.

0597 A velvet touch in the bedroom gives it a stroke of sophistication. Smooth in texture and appearance, it expresses warmth and exudes elegance. Use this material on the headboard to achieve a luxurious environment.

0598 Renoir, a bed by Noir, is completely upholstered in smooth hide. The small legs can be made of chromed or gilded steel. Its smooth shapes and its proximity to the floor invite lying down and enjoying its comfort.

0599 Zanotta's Caracalla bed boasts brushed steel legs. The padded headboard and base are upholstered with polyurethane or polyester fibers. The leather cover is non-removable.

0600 The most characteristic aspect of this bed by Noir is its similarity to a chaise longue. Its white-ice tone is in keeping with the rest of the room, and its gigantic rounded chaise longue structure gives the room a French salon look.

0601 White leather for a bed? Why not? In the bedroom, white serves to convey relaxation and enhance rest, making it a logical choice. The curvy design enhances the calming effect.

0597

0598

0599

0600

0601

0602

0603

0604

0605

0606

0607

0602 A bench at the foot of the bed offers both a place to sit and storage for linen. It also adds a special touch to the bedroom's look. Both the Flint bed and the bench are designed by Rodolfo Dordoni for Minotti.

0603 This design forgoes a headboard in favor of including a small laptop desk adjacent to the bed, in a practical and aesthetically pleasing manner.

0604 Although it is not essential, a chair can be of great use in the bedroom. It can be used to create a reading area or can make for an improvised nightstand.

0605 More than just a decorative accent, a bench at the foot of the bed provides for seating and storage. Available in any style and finish, whether upholstered or wooden, it can help finish off your bedroom's look.

0606 Any corner of the room can be used as a work area. The space created by this glass table with eye-catching legs is complemented by a shelf and a table lamp to provide a comfortable work environment.

0607 The small desk in this bedroom could easily be transformed into a dressing table if a beautiful mirror were to be placed above it.

0608 Given their diminuitive size, nightstands are the ideal piece for adding a touch of color to the room. Before choosing a color, analyze the room's palette and consider what tone can complement and emphasize the dominant range.

0609 This small antique style cupboard has greater versatility than the typical bedside table. The piece boasts a spacious interior, and its surface is the ideal place on which to place a reading lamp and some books.

0610 Creating a bedside table from antique style wooden boxes is not only an ecological solution, it also gives the room an original touch. The boxes can stack up until they achieve the desired height, and they can be painted and decorated. The result is eclectic chic at its best.

0611 In some cases, the bed's own structure has a built-in bedside table on each side. This option represents a saving of space and homogenizes the decoration, but, on the other hand, it does not allow the small table to be the contrast that enriches the room's style.

0612 Through the paint effects, moldings and ornamental details of the matching headboard and side table a maritime theme is created. This theme is enhanced by many of the room's accessories.

0613 If the bedroom is classically styled, opt for a traditional bedside table design. In addition to presenting an aesthetic complement to the room, its shelves add storage capacity.

0614 A simple white cube, a sort of dice whose numbers are missing, can function perfectly as a bedside table in a chic environment. In this bedroom, the geometric shapes help acheive the desired sophistication.

0615 Bedside tables can be the unexpected detail with which to create an original atmosphere, because just about any object with a flat surface can be used.

0608

0609

0610

0611

0612

0613

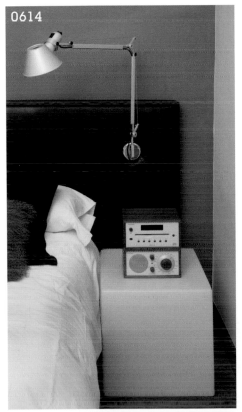

0614

0615

0616 To take advantage of the space below the window, you can position a narrow chest of drawers. It is a way of distributing storage areas to lighten the wardrobe's content and to keep frequently needed items at hand.

0617 In this warm bedroom, a wooden chest with grilled doors substitutes as a bedside table, combining multiple uses into one beautiful, practical piece.

0618 Here two stacked suitcases have been used as a sort of bedside table. They display patterns that cheer the room up and offer two useful spaces: the interiors and the top surface. It is an original idea that helps to settle the problem of selecting side tables for low-to-the-ground beds.

0619 In addition to being decorative and functional for a bedroom, a chest of drawers is at much at home in the dining room, living room or kitchen, so that it could be used in a different room in the future, once a change in style is desired.

0620 A piece of furniture with a multitude of drawers lets space be compartmentalized and contents organized in a simple way. This industrial looking chest of drawers emphasizes space division through the use of different colors for the drawers.

0621 When a bedroom contains multiple elements that each have a distinct personality, with multiple textures and styles, make sure to view a prospective piece, such as this side table, in situ before finalizing the purchase, to ensure the elements cohere well.

0622 Add some wheels to any furniture and you will get maximum versatility. Bedside tables with wheels are extremely practical: you can move them closer to the bed in order to reach something or to clean easily underneath.

0623 In a minimalist space, consider including a low, light-colored wooden table with geometric lines. The grained texture provides a nature-inspired element in the heart of the room.

0616

0617

0618

0619

0620

0621

0622

0623

0624 If you don't mind renouncing the functionality of a shelved bedside table for the sake of an artistic statement in your bedroom, a surprising idea is to substitute it with a dramatic piece of art, such as this sculpture. And if the upper surface is flat as in this example, you can at least place a lamp upon it.

0625 If the area is so reduced that there is no room for placing a table on each side of the bed, there are several objects that can exercise a similar function. A small stool, for example, allows for basic objects on its surface.

0626 Wood conveys warmth, a very appropriate quality for a bedroom. Any furniture can be made of wood: the bed's structure, the bedside table, even the lamp! Organic and pleasant, this material will help to create a welcoming atmosphere in which to give oneself over to sleep.

0627

0628

0629

0630

0627 If you like leaving things in view, you can consider substituting the typical bedside table for a long shelf. The total storage space will be less than that of a piece of furniture with drawers or various shelves, but keeping only the basic items will be sufficient and these will function as decorative elements.

0628 A small table slightly taller than the bed is of the appropriate height for placing a reading lamp that allows you to read comfortably.

0629 To protect a wooden table top from scratches and stains, an option is to place a glass laminate upon the table top. In this way you will be able to leave a glass of water on the bedside table without worrying about it damaging the material.

0630 If you have no storage problems, you can consider the option of placing a decorative rather than functional bedside table. This small and slender table top with a bureau style is the ideal surface on which to place elements that give the room life.

0631

0632

0633

0634

0635

0636

0637

0631 Even though reaching its surface from the bed is nearly impossible, a column of various drawers means a functional and versatile way of taking advantage of the space.

0632 One of the bedroom's main furnishings, the bedside table, becomes your ally for managing to give the atmosphere a determined style. In this case, the small vintage table enhances the room's welcoming and intimate environment

0633 This cream colored piece of furniture without handles creates a space with a classic look, turning a simple chest into a sort of dreamy dressing table when combined with the vintage mirror.

0634 There are pieces of furniture that tred the line between table and chair, between shelf and sculpture. Versatile and apt for any space, they can exercise infinite functions. If we place them in a bedroom, they can be used as a decorative and mobile bedside table.

0635 Designed by Bertelé Mobili, this chest of drawers is handpainted and boasts pearl handles. Inspired by the 18th-century Venetian style, this work of art is appropriate for highlighting an environment's refined character.

0636 The Harvey chest of drawers has a dark brown wooden base, drawers with a shining lacquered finish and sophisticated black nickel details. Designed by Rudolph Dordoni for Minotti, its volume evokes Scandinavian chests of drawers from the 1970s.

0637 The pouf is an ideal accessory for a low bed or futon. In addition to being mobile and looking good in any room, if you place it at the side of the futon it can be used as a bedside table. Also, this comfortable seat enhances the elegant style of the bedroom's Asian look.

0638 In addition to making good use of space, an advantage of a pull-out wardrobe is comfort. The fact that the wardrobe, including its bars, shelves and other storage systems, can be pulled out facilitates the organization of the contents and provides easy access.

0639 Relatively little space is needed to include a dressing room. Between a wooden door and some opaque glass windows, a narrow area is hidden while including many storage options. Besides facilitating the arrangement of clothes, this area is wide enough to get dressed in.

0640 If the closet's interior is critical, the outside is no less important. The doors are the ideal surface to give the bedroom a decorative touch, or, as in this case, a youthful look. Apply an adhesive vinyl to change the appearance of an otherwise neutral closet.

0641 Designed by Besana, the Domino wardrobe owes its name to its upholstered black leather doors that look like domino pieces. Attractive and playful, this voluminous wardrobe has sliding doors.

0642 Before choosing a wardrobe, there is a decision you have to make. Do you want it with or without doors? If the content needs heavy organization, the best option is the doorless wardrobe, even though it has a disadvantage: dust. The visual effect of a doorless wardrobe is, however, stunning.

0642

0643

0644

0645

0646

0647

0648

0649

0650

0643 If you only have one wardrobe, its inner distribution needs to be calculated with precision and provide for different types of storage. You will need vertical areas for hanging garments like trousers and dresses, and horizontal spaces like shelves or drawers, in order to store clothes that can be folded.

0644 In order to be able to change the arrangement according to varying needs over time, adjustable wardrobe shelves are recommended. Another aspect you need to take into account when setting up the shelves is the kind of garments you are going to store on these shelves for better organization.

0645 One of the most important qualities in a wardrobe is its versatility. This sideboard by Cia International is a good example of functionality both for its structure and its organization. Symmetrical and easily movable, it is adapted to any corner of the bedroom.

0646 Designed by Jesse, the original Plurimo wardrobe suits a variety of contemporary lifestyles. With a composite versatility that ensures maximum flexibility, the Breeze doors are made of lacquered brushed pinewood.

0647 The Flou wardrobe presents six options of polished glass doors with bronze printing, an elegant and tasteful addition to any contemporary bedroom.

0648 Storage, designed by Piero Lissoni in collaboration with Porro, is a modular system that allows for the display of stored items. Its beautiful design dresses up a room.

0649 The most important item in a bedroom is the bed, and so we need to prevent the wardrobe from usurping its prominence. These discrete doors, although tastefully decorative, hide the storage area without attracting undue attention.

0650 The Dossier DC290M wardrobe's doors, designed by Pinuccio Borgonovo for Former, feature an interesting system of movement: they fold, pivot and finally slide back, offering complete access to the interior

0651 These spotlights that hang from the ceiling like golden bells demonstrate that often the function of a lamp is not simply to light up a room, but also to contribute to the creation of the desired ambiance. The matt golden finish and the way the fixture emits light add to this room's décor.

0652 During the night, this floor lamp emits full spectrum lighting, which is known as the type of lighting that best mimics the natural qualities of daylight.

0653 General lighting is insufficient for carrying out some activities in the bedroom. It is necessary to set up other light sources to reinforce ambient lighting and to be able to read comfortably.

0654 To read in bed, lighting must not be glaring. It should not cast shadows on the book either. A lamp with a diffuser on the bedside table is the best option because it provides good reading lighting.

0655 The EC 400 table lamp consists of a thin copper body that oscillates above a square nickel base. A single 1-watt LED diode emits a diffused beam over a fairly wide area. The lamp was designed by Enzo Catellani design for Catellani &Smith.

0656 This wall-mounted swing-arm light fixture is absolutely ideal for bedroom lighting. This design is extremely versatile and since it is wall-mounted, the bedside table is clear for other items.

0657 In this bedroom with black walls, the common nightstand lamp has been replaced with a decorative hanging light fixture. It provides enough lighting for the bed area, and since it does not produce any glare, it makes for the perfect reading lamp.

0658 On this low bedside table, the lamp emits indirect and smooth lighting to promote relaxation. Its minimalist design fits nicely next to a decorative African mask. As for colors, the contrast between black and white is softened by the light.

0651

0653

0652

0654

0655

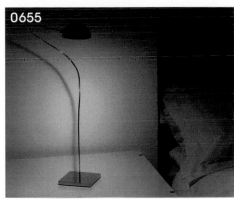

0656

0657

0658

0659 Before you choose bedroom lamps, think about what type of lighting you need and what your priorities are. If reading is not an essential activity in this room, a lamp on the headboard side will mainly be decorative and provide ambient lighting.

0660 Lov is a round shaped wall lamp with a matt white aluminum structure. Designed by Nahtrang Disseny for LEDS-C4, this reading light fixture has two 4-volt and one 3-volt LEDs.

0661 Pleg is a folding wall-mounted lamp made of wood veneer forming a shell. This design from Yonoh studio for LZF Lamps won the Red Dot Design Award 2012.

0662 This Tobias Grau design was baptized with a poetic name: Falling Star. As a shooting star, this wall lamp offers a playful approach to light. Thanks to the LED technology it emits an intense, adjustable, low consumption light.

0663 Designed by R&S Comelissen for Lucente, Amrak is an aluminum cone shape wall lamp. When directing the light downward, this spotlight draws attention toward the bedside table and highlights its presence inside the bedroom.

0659

0660

0661

0663

0662

0664

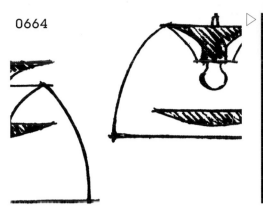

0665

0666

0667

0664 The great advantage of the Bossinha lamp, designed by Fernando Prado for Lumini, is that it allows light intensity to change by moving the shade up and down. Also, this hanging aluminum lamp includes a cover that provides efficient anti-glare control.

0665 Designed by Javier Herrero for LZF Lamps, the Raindrop lamp owes its name to its shape: it looks like a delicate drop of water that creates a warm and inviting atmosphere. Light emanates from a glass globe and shines through the lampshade made of wood veneer.

0666 A bedroom needs two types of lighting: general lighting and task lighting. This convenient wall-mounted LED diode can almost go unnoticed when tucked into its case during the day.

0667 Scar-LED 1FDS by Trizo21 is a subtle wall-mounted lamp that provides sufficient light for reading without disturbing the surroundings. The flexible tube adds a decorative touch to the lamp and allows light to be directed toward the desired direction.

0677 Play with bold colors against neutral shades to make the bed the focal point in the bedroom. The strong contrast produces a dynamic effect that does not necessarily conflict with the desired restful atmosphere.

0678 Matching pillows is recommended to achieve a clean look. The turquoise pillow and the stripped blue, brown and gold stand out from the white bedspread and bring an elegant feel to the room.

0679 There are designs that make a favorite accessory out of pillows. These items have the capacity to soften a room: here the pattern, pale colors and soft textures combile to create a feminine and romantic style.

0680 To achieve this artful, inspiring look, try to combine colors and textures in a unique way: the smoothness of the velvet contrasts with the saturation of the colors.

0681 Linen offers the flexibility that furniture cannot provide. Experiment with your favorite colors! You can always go back to a more neutral look, but you don't want to miss the chance to explore and create something new.

0682 If you want to personalize children's rooms so that they have a more playful look, be creative with the pillows. Even though they are white, the shapes and the stitching are original.

0677

0679

0678

0680

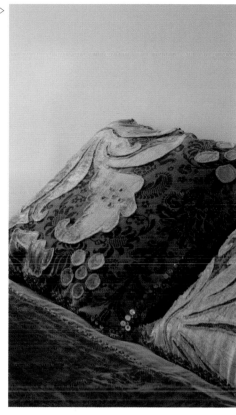

0681

0682

0691 The Jaipur collection by Gancedo is a reinterpretation of the "toile de Jouy." This pattern features landscapes and figures on a soft-colored background.

0692 In order to create a homogenous décor, stick to the same range of colors used on the walls and curtains. Use similar shades for the headboard, the bedspread and the pillows.

0693 To give the bedroom a unique character, you can use a pattern that imitates an animal skin. Animal prints provide the room with a focal point, while adding an exotic touch.

0691

0692

0693

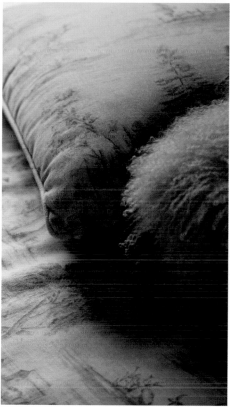

0694 Sometimes we don't need a striking color to enliven a bedroom. The material might just do the trick. A furry pillow, for example, stands out, bringing visual and tactile interest.

0695 The layering of blankets and bedspreads brings the room an attractive combination of textures and tones.

0696 A pillow with different designs on each of its sides is the epitome of versatility. Change it around according to your state of mind to instantly change the décor of your bedroom.

0697

0698

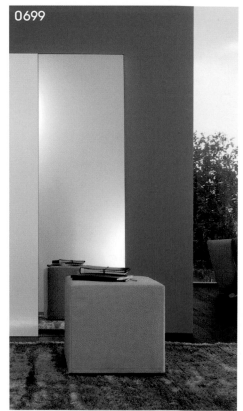

0699

0700

0701

0702

0703

0704

0705

0697 If space allows, a dressing table and desk add flexibility and functionality to the bedroom. The options are infinite!

0698 A bookshelf serves not only as a necessary piece of furniture if you need to include a study area inside the bedroom, rather it can also be used for organizing the room.

0699 Poufs are one of the most versatile furnishings. Soft and springy, they make for comfortable seating. They can also be firm enough to be used as a low table. This elegant pouf is a design of Maximilian Momati for Jesse.

0700 Mirrors are a small space's great allies. The design of this ornate oval mirror seems to be inspired by some fairy tale and gives the room an imaginary look, while it visually expands the space.

0701 You can hang artwork above the headboard to reinforce the bed as the centerpiece in your bedroom.

0702 Wooden crates and boxes can come in handy to create an original side table that also serves for storing books and magazines. Left in their original state or painted, they are a clever and budget-friendly decorating idea.

0703 The dresser does not only fulfill a storage function, it can also be a key item to define a room's style. This black piece of furniture provides plenty of shelf and drawer space and adds an ethnic touch to the bedroom.

0704 If you are looking for a place to hang your collection of scarves or other clothing items, a simple and practical idea is to lean a ladder against a wall. It is without doubt a very creative storage solution.

0705 If you want to install a television in the bedroom, think carefully about the height at which you want it. TV screens come with wall brackets that allow you to mount the device on the wall and be tilted as needed for a better viewing angle.

0706 One of the accessories to take into account for decorating a crib is the cushions. Here the fabric's reddish, orange and yellow colors, combined in this girl's room, overflow with optimism and vitality. With these the generation of a stimulating atmosphere is achieved.

0707 Laser cutting is used to manufacture furniture. This technique is ideal for making personalized items such as this crib. Painted white, it easily integrates in the room, letting the bold decorations stand out.

0708 Wood brings warmth to the littlest ones' rooms. Its natural quality, even in themed designs, generates an ideal atmosphere for rest. Its combination with the headboard's cast iron and the mosquito net recreate a comfortable space with rural atmosphere.

0709 The overuse of white tones can give rise to cold and isolated atmospheres. You have to introduce tones and textures that contrast and break the room's uniformity, for example, the bed's accessories like teddy bears and the colorful striped bedspread.

0706

0707

0708

0709

0710 The orange colored monochromatic decoration confers an active, radiant and expressive character. Bunk beds can be the solution to space problems, since they accommodate children in a single bedroom, optimize the square footage and allow them to have a play area.

0711 This modern and slightly futuristic design includes a bed in the upper part and a desk in the lower part. This is a practical solution for children's bedrooms with little space. The bi-color design in red and black lends a sophisticated touch to the decoration.

0712 The rose color against a neutral tone is common in rooms designed for young girls. Together with the butterfly and fairy designs a calm and comfortable atmosphere is achieved, appropriate for this age bracket. The bed's accessories follow this theme.

0713 This whimsical mosquito net suspended above the bed makes the room into a really original space with a touch of chic. The cute side table matches the bed frame and includes a mobile tray as its tabletop.

0714 Today a wide variety of styles and shapes of nest beds exists: space saving ones, pull along ones, compact ones, ones with drawers, etc. This model includes storage underneath.

0715 This is a nest bed with the mattress base in the upper part and an area with sofas in the lower part. The ladder with drawers at back is another storage solution that takes advantage of the space. The pastel colors give the design vitality and a sense of fun.

0716 If a traditional bed and frame are preferred, it is best to situate it right into the corner of the room, perhaps under a window to take advantage of natural light, in order to save space in the rest of the room for furniture such as a table, chest or bookshelf.

0717

0718

0719

0717 In contrast with complementary colors or in combination with primaries, green bestows a natural feel upon a room. It generates a relaxed atmosphere for children and produces an elegant look. This innovative bed design includes drawers underneath the mattress base, to accomodate extra storage.

0718 The rose color conveys romanticism and is ideal for a vibrant girls' space; this strong tone evokes fun and fantasy. The nest beds joined to the wall are a sure bet, since they include structures with different heights In which chests of drawers and wardrobes have been installed.

0719 The neutral tones of this design give the space great visual span, making it an excellent solution for small children's rooms.

0720 This pleasant piece of furniture designed by P'kolino combines a table and seat and is perfect for children. The design is simple, well balanced and functional, with ample space for paper, books and jigsaw puzzles, echoing the simplicity of the padded seat and storage area below.

0721 Stools are spare furniture that are easy to move and transform. They are an ideal accessory for rooms without a lot of space because they function as a seat or as a footrest. A stool built with different colored and textured fabrics creates an ideal atmosphere for playing and entertainment.

0722 Chests of drawers in children's desks offer the opportunity to give the room a touch of design and color. These pieces of spare furniture are ideal for keeping order, stimulating imagination and having everything at hand.

0723 This unique table and chair set by P'kolino combines fascinating shapes and lines with an overall streamlined look. The addition of a playful rug and fun accessories completes the design.

0724 For this playroom, whimsy and an incredible sense of fun were the inspiration for the unique and child-friendly design. The solid wood pieces combine nicely with the plastic-covered foam pieces, all of which are easy to clean.

0720

0721

0722

0724

0723

0725 Dearkids produces beautiful custom desks that are perfectly adapted to the necessities of children's rooms. The dynamic and energetic character of the room's design is ideal for lively kids.

0726 A round table is ideal for preventing bumps and scrapes, with its lack of sharp corners. The rainbow striped carpet is perfect for adding a splash of color to this otherwise traditional design.

0727 Curvy, contemporary furnishings in a light wood tone lend a feeling of spaciousness to this simple, modern design.

0728 The pleasant color palette in this room is created through the mixing of plain wood, light yellow and natural green. Note the ample storage space and modern lines.

0729 This unit is constructed of ash wood that features a contrast between the cocoa, rose and fuchsia colors. It maximizes storage space while providing a comfortable and dynamic workspace.

0730 This attractive sliding door wardrobe is equipped with a large storage capacity chest and various drawers located on the inside. The overall effect is a compact and highly functional unit.

0731 Multifunctional furniture is the best ally for decorating a small children's room. The sliding drawers and trunks function as storage elements for keeping games and clothes. They are easy pieces of furniture to transform and situate in any corner.

0732 When the smallest children start getting dressed by themselves, built-in wardrobes with frame and curtain are a very practical option, as long as they are appropriate in height.

0733 Refurbished antique furniture gives a personal touch to any bedroom. The wood's natural and always elegant color is a classic style choice; the pieces of sturdy wood instill an authentic luxury so that the room's occupant feels comfortable.

0734 This wardrobe displays a pleasant tri-color combination that is repeated in the whole room's design. Vibrant color is one of the easiest ways to enliven a room.

0735 This lacquered wardrobe with four large sliding doors, in tones of yellow and orange, creates an interplay of contrasts underlined by horizontal lines. In the interior, the wardrobe is equipped with large capacity drawers and suspended clothes rack hangers. An ideal design for children.

0730

0731

0732

0733

0734

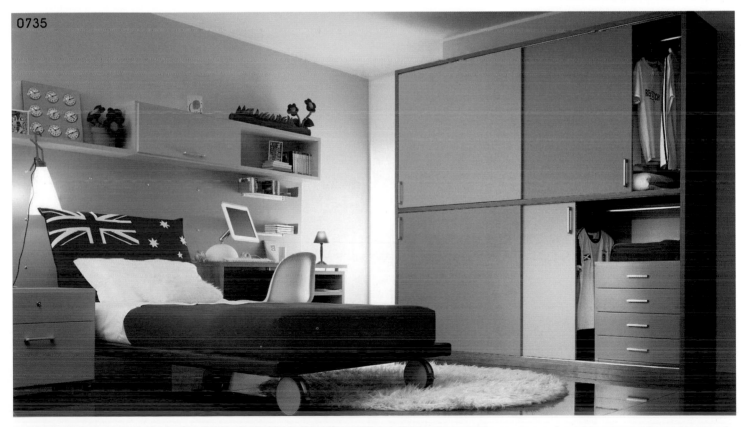

0735

0736 Wicker is characterized by its warmth, being a material of natural origin. Thus wicker baskets are a classic for baby room design, as well as a practical storage element.

0737 Shelves are a highly important element to maintain order. They can also double as decorative elements. In this case, some old treated and refurbished boxes are used as storage for games and books.

0738 These lacquered shelves with foldable doors are an effective resource for children's rooms. This system allows quick use and a perfect place for storing books and toys. In this case, a shade of saffron has been chosen as the ideal color for the space.

0739 The purpose of storage boxes may be utilitarian, but that's no reason to waste their potential as a decorative object. Wood is a resistant and very durable material and it is easy to paint and decorate to the child's taste.

0740 The storage in this nest bed is a great solution to the problem of tight spaces. Generally with nest beds, the storage spaces are located in the lower area, to allow easy access. The blue and green color scheme is soothing and restful.

0741 Dearkids' use of stairs with built-in storage stands out for its practicality and innovation. Elevated bed systems already maximize space by leaving the space underneath open for use, and in this case the additional utility of the piece is just outstanding.

0742 Among the many storage boxes on the market today, these metal ones stand out. They have a retro style and display very diverse colors. The lids can double as trays.

0743 The best solution for taking advantage of an alcove in the wall is the placement of stacks of shelves. The shelves help organize clutter and are useful for placing either toys or books. It is essential that they be placed at an appropriate height for children.

0736

0737

0738

0739

0740

0741

0742

0743

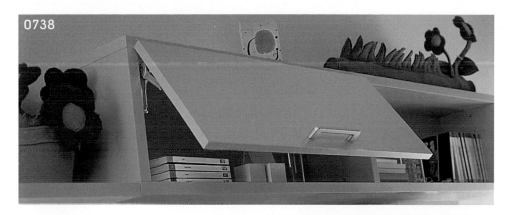

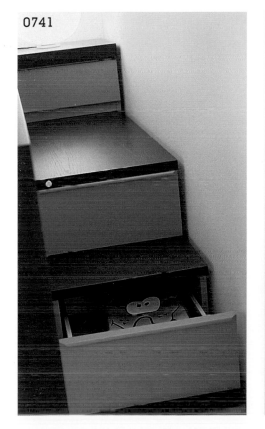

0744 Creative solutions that make tidying the bedroom efficient and fun help encourage children to keep things in their place.

0745 Becoming familiar with the effects that different colors have on our moods will help in deciding what tones are most appropriate for children's rooms. Reds and oranges are inviting, stimulating and cheerful.

0746 Plush toys made of adorable animal shapes are ideal for decorating any room, and they let the smallest children play and stimulate their imagination.

0747 If space allows for a small wooden swing to be installed in a child's room, consider including this whimsical piece, but be sure to have it professionally installed following all safety regulations.

0744

0745

0746

0747

0748

0749

0750

0751

0752

0748 The red and white theme evokes the joyfulness of childhood. Choosing a vibrant color scheme for both the bedspread and accessories is a bold move, but design for children is the time to make fun selections.

0749 In adult bedrooms, an excess of cushions seems too busy and over the top. But in design for children, there's no such thing as too many soft, fun cushions.

0750 Custom made children's cushions delight even the smallest kids. These accessories are useful and decorative, and allow the children to play and let their imaginations fly away with them.

0751 The color blue, in all its extensive chromatic range, transmits calm. It is the color of the infinite, of dreams, and evokes rest. When combined with other colors, such as this embroidered detailing, the effect is stunning.

0752 In this room the combination of the wall's rosy and cream tones, the bedclothes, the cushions and the accessories generate a perfect visual harmony. These colors may be a conventional choice for girls' rooms, but the effect is classic and fun.

0753 Lamps of white colored spherical shapes are a modern choice for any type of children's room. During the day they are very decorative and by night they create an effective atmospheric light. In general, these lamps are made out of polyethylene resin.

0754 Adjustable light fixtures, such as reading lamps, are ideal for placing above a desk. Care has to be taken with materials that are put within children's reach and to avoid the fluorescent tubes. These designs are flexible, functional and very original.

0755 Lanterns provide a fun lighting solution. This type of light, located in strategic points, allows you to attend to the child during the night without disturbing them. These minimalist style designs are easily transportable.

0756 The design of this lamp for desks or games tables emits the perfect amount of light to facilitate stimulation, learning and games.

0753

0754

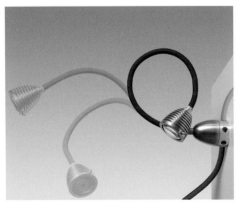

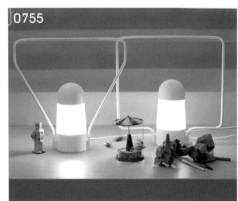
0755

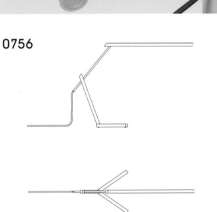
0756

0757 Decorating kids' rooms with self-adhesive vinyl wall decorations brings life, color and imagination. It is an economical solution and takes children to a world of fantasy and fun. Tree and animal designs are the most successful for the décor of children's spaces.

0758 With a simple cord, like a clothes line, you can create a useful solution for hanging photos or artwork, or whatever the child considers most important. You have to take into account that the wall must be monochromatic in order not to overload the decoration.

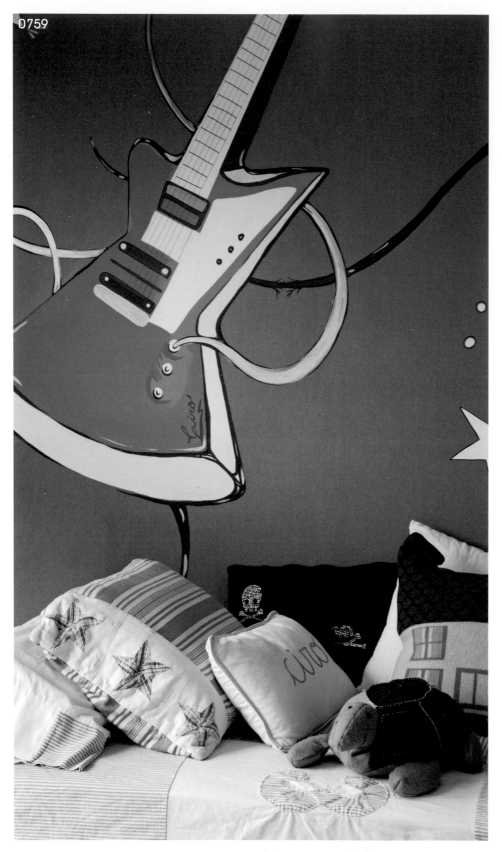

0759

0760

0761

0762

0763

0764

0765

0759 Murals give a very original touch to any children's room, filling them with fantasy and tenderness and allowing the children to give a free rein to their imagination and to their capacity for play. For example, with a guitar and some painted stars we reflect the child's dreamy personality in their surroundings.

0760 Decorative vinyls are very versatile and can often serve an educational purpose as well as decoration, such as a world map.

0761 Wall pegs bring the order and organization necessary in kids' rooms. Displaying pictures above the pegs brings a sense of fun to that corner of the room.

0762 In this case, a short clothes line on the wall is a very original and practical resource for showcasing personal items as a decorative element.

0763 The rustic style of this room is acheived by a simple picture frame and stack of shelves in combination with the room's traditional wood furniture.

0764 In babies' rooms it is very common to use the wall for placing photos of the first milestones in life. White multi-frames are a solution that, combined with the perfect wall color, can be highly effective.

0765 If toys and teddy bears are important elements that accompany children during their growth, hanging them on the wall facilitates the child having them at hand. Constructed of a simple cord, this version provides a touch of originality to the room's design.

0766 Ensuite bathrooms are no longer a luxury. Whether it is a new construction or a remodel, a modern home is becoming a versatile space where partitions are kept to a minimum. This often affects the layout of the bedroom, which can openly incorporate the bathroom.

0767 An open shower offers a whole range of possibilities: To start with, the flooring is continuous throughout with no level change. Since there are no enclosures, shower heads and other shower-related plumbing fixtures gain visual importance.

0768 The Arne ergonomic bathtub made of white titanic resin stands out for its sinuous shape that pays homage to the Egg chair designed by Arne Jacobsen in 1958 for the Radisson SAS hotel in Copenhagen.

0769 The Deque line of bath and spa faucet by Dornbracht is easily recognized by its flat, wide spout that spills a gentle rain-like flow of water. This severe design rounds off a minimalist bathroom design.

0770 Lavasca is an elegant bathtub in titanic resin conceived by Matteo Thun for Studio Rapsel. Elegant and sculptural, the Lavasca tub has paved its way to the Philadelphia Art Museum permanent contemporary design collection.

0766

0767

0768

0769

0770

0771 This bathtub and floor mount bath filler express a fusion between old and new in industrial design. The shape of the bathtub with its curvaceous form references the old slipper tub popular during the Victorian era. One end is raised and sloped to provide greater back support.

0772 This wall mounted shower head in brushed stainless steel designed by Studio Rapsel is a minimalist design choice that elegantly contrasts with the rich grain pattern of the wood panel.

0773 An overhead shower and hand shower combo has turned what was once a simple shower into pure luxury: the overhead shower releases a lavish spray of water that feels just like rain, while the hand shower fulfills more directed showering needs.

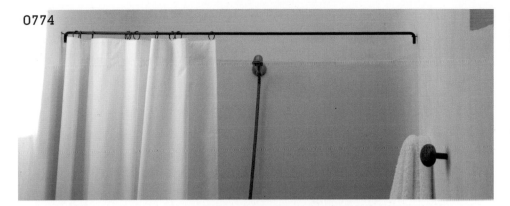

0774

0775

0776

0774 A limited color palette, straightforward lines and subtle detailing create an austere ambiance that transmits a sense of balance, serenity and harmony. Good natural lighting is the finishing touch that ties together a simple bathroom.

0775 This built-in bathtub is framed by a dark wood ledge, creating contrast with the white tub and walls and reinforcing the country style of the bathroom. The white river stones and the exposed ceiling beams introduce a natural touch in line with the style of the room.

0776 Concrete is a popular material, especially in contemporary home design. Its rich texture brings visual interest and creates a warm and inviting atmosphere or a cool and industrial look depending on the materials it is combined with.

0777

0778

0779

0780

0781

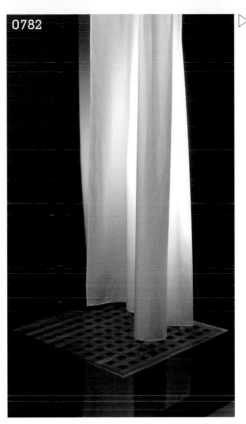

0782

0783

0777 The first thought that might come to your mind when looking at this stainless steel bathtub may be that of coldness. In fact, stainless steel is the best material for a tub because it keeps the water warm the longest!

0778 KeaVasca is another modern interpretation of the slipper bathtub, which has an inclined back allowing for maximum comfort as you bathe the hours of stress away. Instead of claw feet, the bathtub has an integrated base giving the overall design a monolithic look.

0779 Designer Matteo Thun conceived this clever shower system that combines a spiraled curtain rail and shower head. Playful yet elegant, the Pluviae system creates a distinct circular space rather than the typical rectangular shower.

0780 Show off your style and make a design statement with plumbing fixtures and faucets. Oil-rubbed bronze fixtures are a popular choice thanks to the vintage trend and are a good match for your claw-foot tub.

0781 Studio Rapsel's Cobra wall-mounted shower is made of satin stainless steel. This unique contemporary shower system allows for a distinctive minimalist profile that meets the highest standards in bathroom design.

0782 The main advantage that a built-in shower tray offers is that it can be flush with the bathroom floor allowing for a continuous surface. The tray is made of genuine teak, a material containing a natural oil that repels water and keeps the wood from warping.

0783 A built-in concrete bathtub goes nicely with the rough plastered walls for a rustic country style. Natural materials and an abundance of textures evoke images of a seaside cottage.

0784 The rc40 sink unit by Burgbad is made of a material that matches the wall finish. It brings an architectural aesthetic to the design of this bathroom, diverging from traditional bathroom furnishings.

0785 This counter-mounted single-handle faucet designed around a sleek cylinder makes a refreshing statement in a bathroom where rich patina finishes dominate. Also, the curve of the spout relates to the soft shape of the vessel.

0786 In this innovative master bedroom, the vanity takes center stage. Sleek white cabinets form the vanity base, while the washbasins are seamlessly integrated into the design.

0787 The Crystalline line of basins by Alape is fabricated of enameled steel, which makes them very durable. The high gloss finish gives the pieces a certain lightness and delicacy. Standing or wall-mounted, the basins are accompanied by drawers.

0788 An architectural approach to bathroom design is achieved by introducing modules, whose variations accommodate solutions for almost any type of space and need.

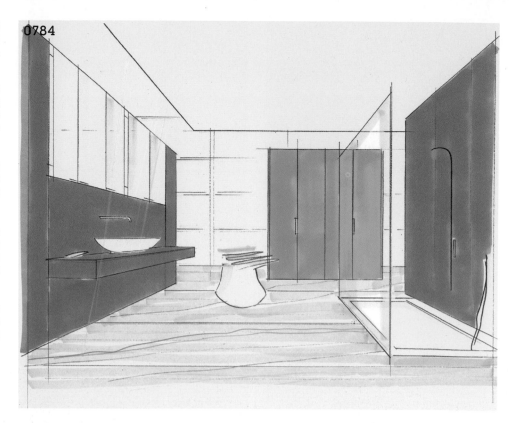

0786

0787

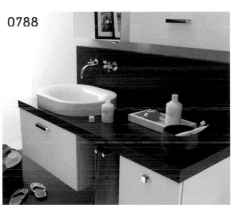

0788

0789 Carmen Barasona created this water inspired hotel bathroom design. The soft lines of the basins are suggestive of river stones, eroded over time by the continuous flow of running water.

0790 The wall-mounted washbasin adds to the airiness of the bathroom. All the plumbing fixtures are white and become an integral part of the bathroom design. In contrast, the movable storage cabinet and over the counter tray are of wood.

0791 This rounded surface-mounted ceramic washbasin recalls a polished pebble. It makes a minimalist statement lending a simplicity and serenity to the bathroom. This effect is reinforced by the soft gray tile on the walls and on the washbasin console.

0789

0790

0791

0792

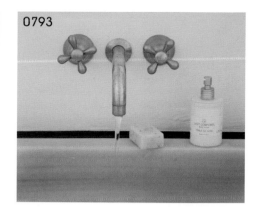

0793

0794

0795

0792 A neutral color scheme was chosen to combine a salvaged marble basin and wood console table, creating a vintage look. In contrast, the contemporary fittings introduce a modern twist to the overall design.

0793 At first glance, this mismatched anodized steel spout and vintage style nickel handles seem like a strange combination. Nonetheless this mix picks up on the cool and warm shades of the marble sink.

0794 Upgrading a bathroom does not always require a total makeover, especially when there are budget constraints. You can achieve a different feel by simply replacing the faucets with some reasonably priced fixtures.

0795 Combining the traditional look of marble with a contemporary wall-mounted faucet gives this bathroom an up-to-date yet timeless design.

0796 Nothing makes guests feel more pampered than a stylish powder room. A block of rough marble for the basin, and an antique-cut crystal chandelier and oval mirror punch up a small room.

0797 A gilded recessed sink and copper faucet add character to this bathroom infused with a warm glow provided by the yellow tone of the walls. The faucet was mounted to one side due to the limited depth of the counter.

0798 Like regular concrete, fibered concrete can be shaped in any desired way, and can also be stained in a wide variety of colors to match the décor of a room.

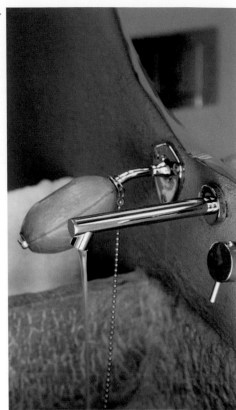

0799

0800

0801

0799 This antique marble sink is supported between two flanking ledges, leaving a space underneath for storage. This is a clever design that works with the rustic style of the room without compromising comfort and functionality.

0800 Accessorize the area around your washbasin according to the style of the room. For instance, antique silver vessels and perfume flasks were chosen to go with a marble wainscoat and mirror frame, and a sink with brass legs.

0801 Straight lines are dominant in this bathroom, including the tubular faucet spout. The contrasting stone wall behind the frameless mirror and polished finishes is visually striking.

0802 This rough block vessel, rustic and clean-lined, along with the sandy tones of the vanity and walls, would go perfectly in a simple beachside cabin.

0803 Portuguese architect Eduardo Souto de Moura is mostly known for his extraordinary buildings and his attention to materials and detail. The same attention is translated to the design of pieces such as this freestanding cylindrical washbasin in travertine.

0804 This stone vessel on a wood counter is displayed as an art object. Its sculptural quality is unmistakable.

0805 A freestanding vanity with a mirror sections off an area of the room. More than a functional item, it is an important design element that organizes the circulation around the room.

0806 The soft brushed finish of the faucet complements the Corian sink. This is an example of how high-tech products can create a warm, natural feel.

0807

0808

0809

0810

0807 The Diva line by Burgbad is feminine and full of nostalgia for 1940s-style furniture. The washstand consists of an oval chest of drawers topped with a stone basin. This luxurious piece has golden feet and a drawer handle inlaid with Swarovski crystals.

0808 This bathroom design makes the most of a corner window, under which the bathtub is built. Bathrooms should be places to relax and enjoy rather than a utility room, and viewing windows help acheive this.

0809 The washbasin is an important feature of a bathroom. It may be distinctive and have a striking shape, but ultimately, it should be in harmony with the rest of the room's components.

0810 By providing a faucet-mounting hole on its wide flange, this ceramic basin avoids the hassle of drilling an additional hole in the countertop material.

0811 Whether ceramic, glass, metal, or stone, vessel basins rest perfectly flush atop the counter. Because of this, vessels are easier to replace as opposed to recessed washbasins and can often be showstoppers.

0812 A nice new faucet is sometimes enough to upgrade a bathroom. The arched spout and cross handles of this faucet create a vintage look combined with the plain white tile countertop and backsplash and the wood framed mirror.

0813 This octagonal washbasin featuring stepped sides evokes the style of grand eras past. In the context of a room where wood is the dominant material, the ceramic sink fits elegantly.

0814 A washbasin with an extra wide ledge on one side has a slightly elevated lip to prevent water dripping onto the floor. Its design works particularly well with the beveled subway tiles of the wall.

0811

0812

0813

0814

0815

0816

0817

0818

0815 For a clean and uncluttered décor, wall-mounted faucets are a good choice. Sleek and geometric forms with refined spouts and handles will give a bathroom a splash of style, especially when combined with a light color scheme.

0816 Avoid cluttering your bathroom countertops with toiletries other than soap and a hand towel. Instead consider displaying a simple decoration item such as this freshly picked sprig, to enhance the beauty of the materials used in the room.

0817 Add some texture when a bathroom is too cold and uninviting. Use fabrics such as silk, linen or wool to create a more natural, inviting and agreeable feeling, but avoid too much pattern as this would interfere with the clean look.

0818 A table console with a matching mirror, which was originally part of a bedroom set, is repurposed here to decorate a bathroom. The chipped paint finish is preserved for greater effect.

0819 Contemporary plumbing fixtures, rather than being perceived as cold and bare, should be conceived as fixtures with clean and smooth surfaces that appeal equally to men and women.

0820 Floor mounted tub fillers combine old-world craftsmanship and contemporary high-tech manufacturing. Decorative metal hoses, cross handles and porcelain handle buttons enhance a luxurious and pleasurable bathing experience.

0821 Since privacy is not really a concern when using a washbasin, it can be moved outside the bathroom as long as plumbing allows, for example into the bedroom or dressing room.

0822 A waterfall spout is commonly used as a bathtub filler for its relaxing waterfall flow. Nonetheless, they can be used to fill washbasins with the same calming effect.

0823 Dressing up the deck of an undermount bathtub is a simple way to make a design statement in a bathroom. Whether stone, ceramic or wood, it'll help frame the bathtub, making it the centerpiece of a room.

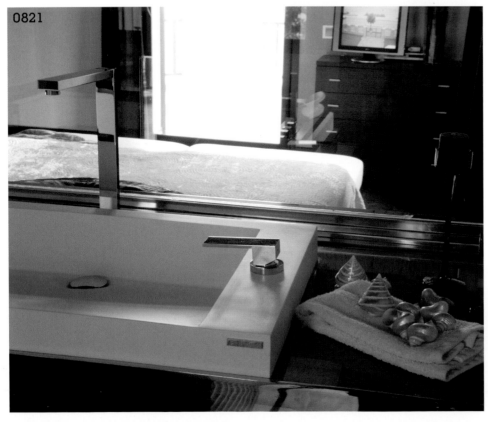

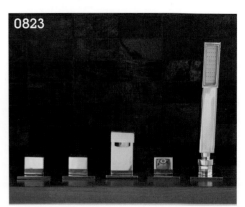

0824

0825

0826

0827

0824 A surface-mounted washbasin adds a decorative note to a bathroom either on its own or combined with a wash top. While they are easier to install than recessed basins, surface-mounted sinks require more care.

0825 This simple geometric washbasin manufactured by Alape, for its Metaphor series of bathroom products, is conceived as a piece of furniture which combines functionality and décor. The glazed steel basin sits on a base of American oak.

0826 Wall-mounted faucets are perfect for vessel sinks. From traditional to modern, there are models to fit any style. These chrome cross handles and gooseneck spout tie together an ultra modern sink and a decorative framed mirror.

0827 This thick concrete shelf incorporates two sinks and makes an architectural statement. Hand-packing the concrete is a method that produces the attractive veining. A coat of polyaspartic is usually applied for protection against water penetration.

0828 A hand-carved stone washbasin can lend a custom look to your bathroom, providing durability and handcrafted beauty. While stone vessels are an expensive option, it is a good investment that will add value to your home.

0829 Try to keep your bathroom counter clutter free to let the material truly shine. Nonetheless, a few carefully chosen items can be used to complement the décor in favor of simplicity and casual elegance.

0830 This old, rough concrete trough equipped with copper spout and handles has an antique country style charm. Since concrete is unpredictable, every piece is unique.

0831 The beveled mirrors, a painted and distressed candle holder and a silver pitcher with dried flowers harmonize with the warm gray of the epoxy finished concrete bathroom countertop.

0832

0833

0834

0835

0836

0832 Leftover fabrics can be handy when you want to refurbish a vanity table. Turn this fabric into a skirt to disguise the underside of the sink or hide unsightly plumbing devices, while adding some charm to the room.

0833 A vanity area is built in an otherwise unusable corner of a room. This is a perfect opportunity to make a design statement, in this case with a particularly nice vessel mounted on a bespoke table.

0834 The sill of a window offers additional surface space behind a bathroom sink. Not exactly flush, the top of the sink is slightly higher than the windowsill. This facilitates the transition between materials.

0835 The counter and walls, which have the same finish, serve as backdrop for a fired ceramic vessel and a matching framed mirror with swing-arm wall lamp. The chrome faucet adds some sparkle and the decorating items bring in a touch of color.

0836 A long wood countertop unifies a vanity area with two vessels, which are accompanied by their respective faucets and ceiling-mounted rotating mirrors. The result is a very functional and airy space.

0837 A slender but strong profile vanity is the beautiful focal point of this bathroom. In this case, it is effectively displayed with a bold color on the walls around it. Scale back the rest of the elements so the overall design of the room isn't overwhelming.

0838 A vanity and matching wall cabinet make up a composition that plays with verticality and horizontality, solid and void, and balance and asymmetry.

0839 Various pieces of furniture were chosen to introduce a warm touch of wood in a room where white dominates. These furniture pieces provide the area around the trough washbasin with storage in a simple but functional composition.

0840 The depth of a counter or vanity doesn't need to be greater than the vessel sink that will go on top of it. This kind of washbasin only requires a small cut out into the support that serves as a drain hole.

0841 Material, texture and color are orchestrated to further articulate the design elements. Far from being dull, monochromatic color schemes in contrast with ultra modern stainless steel fixtures infuse your bathroom with a sophisticated touch.

0842 An interesting looking washbasin can play a major role in setting the tone of your bathroom. This glass washbasin is definitely an attention catcher, reflecting the colors and finishes of the tiles, mirror, fittings and the light.

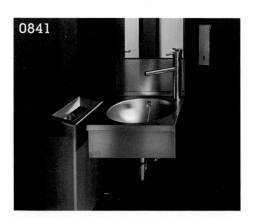

0843

0844

0845

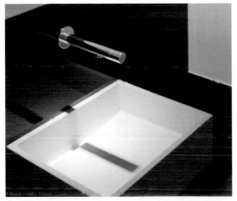

0846

0843 For a small bathroom, avoid bulky units. Instead go for space saving vanities that still offer plenty of storage room, while making a bathroom look larger.

0844 Tatoo is the name of this wall-mounted washbasin in Corian material, with stainless steel towel rail manufactured by Rapsel. Tatoo is the expression of the concept of flow and form reduced to its bare essentials, without neglecting functionality.

0845 Two sinks are very convenient in shared bathrooms, if space allows. Because there are two of them, they will have a greater impact on a bathroom. Lighting and accessories such as mirrors will double in size, and so will storage!

0846 This single lever chrome basin faucet stands out primarily for its aesthetic design, becoming the focus of any bathroom. Its enhanced functionality provides ease of use and greater accessibility.

0847 This mirror slides across the front of this cabinet above the sink. While it hides much of the cabinet, it does leave part of it exposed for easy access without having to maneuver around swinging doors.

0848 Burgbad's Culta mirror cabinet has a fully-mirrored front that lifts up and folds to reveal the interior of the cabinet. It also provides lighting, keeping the lines of a minimalist bathroom tidy.

0849 Burgbad's Solaire line of bathroom furnishings features a striking combination of colors and finishes that can liven up a bland room. The vanity has integrated towel bars, while the mirrored wall cabinet has incorporated lighting.

0850 The Sinea line by Burgbad features furnishings fully equipped with all the necessary accessories and storage possibilities. A shelf with integrated lighting above the mirrored front of the medicine cabinet provides excellent diffused lighting.

0851 In addition to fulfilling their obvious function, the side mirrors flanking the washbasin enhance the décor. Made out of vertical stripes, they create a playful visual effect and open up the space.

0852 Rapsel's Melting Chic line features bathroom furnishings in rosewood. The wall-mounted cabinet has a mirrored front and an open shelf for easy access. The rationalist design is reminiscent of Mondrian's Neo-Plasticism.

0853 This is a wall-mounted mirrored cabinet with hidden lateral shelves manufactured by Rapsel. The volumetric design of this product is enhanced by the material, which creates many reflections.

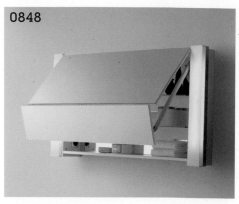

0851

0852

0853

0854

0855

0856

0854 An ornate mirror and light fixture add some detail to a simple bathroom and turn the vanity area into the focal point without altering the bones of the room. This allows the décor of the room to be changed as desired at any given moment.

0855 An alternative to the above-sink medicine cabinet is this wall-mounted column cabinet with a mirrored front. Clearly it doubles as a full-length mirror and can be used in the bedroom or the dressing room.

0856 This recessed cabinet fully integrates into the bathroom. Because of its location down low, it is not suitable for keeping prescriptions out of the reach of children, but it can certainly be used for toiletries.

0857 The Vista wall-mounted mirror manufactured by Rapsel has an LCD 8-inch (20 cm) TV with touch screen buttons, and connections to DVD and cable TV. Perfect for catching the morning news while getting ready for the day.

0858 This convenient cylindrical bathroom cabinet on casters has a top that can be used as a tray and can be wheeled wherever needed: by the shower, tub or washbasin.

0859 Two side column cabinets mark the entry to a bathroom. Their elegant look is an introduction to what comes next: a spacious room with furnishings characterized by clean lines.

0860 A right angle mirror is a pair of plane mirrors adjoined at right angle to each other. It is often used in bathrooms for wraparound reflections and because they make the room look larger and brighter.

0861 Small drawers are piled up to form a large storage unit. Perhaps not the most practical due to the number of drawers and their proportions, it is however suggestive of the Japanese step tansu cabinet and goes nicely with the wood ceiling beams.

0862 Utilitarian vanities feature integrated towel bars on their fronts, sides or both. These additions hold functionality without marring the look of the vanity they are attached to and avoid the necessity of having to mount pegs on the walls.

0863 A glass shelf and shower wall give this bathroom a clean look. The glass shelf keeps bathroom accessories within reach or provides a sleek way for displaying decorative items.

0864 The dark finish of the under counter cabinet imitates the low tiled wall of the bathtub and shower. Colors above the counter line are lighter. By doing this, all the visual weight is kept close to the floor, keeping the upper part airier.

0865 A custom vanity and shelves are the best option to keep a unified design in the bathroom. The sharp contrast with the white surfaces and the rich texture of the wood are the result of the attention to detail.

0863

0864

0865

0866 An open shelf under a vanity counter will come very handy for storage. It is in line with the clean look of the bathroom and camouflages the unsightly drain pipes of the vessels.

0867 Designing a modern bathroom with a vintage look takes careful planning and a bit of research. Priority is given to the major items: bathtub, shower, toilet and washbasin. Then come the accessories that will give the bathroom the desired look.

0868 A pair of traditional metal wall hooks with ceramic tips are the final touch to this unadorned yet functional bathroom. This is proof that there is no need to spend much to create a perfectly functional and visually pleasant space.

0869 If storage space in a bathroom is an issue, take advantage of wall space by hanging towels on a ladder drying rack. Available in many styles and finishes, you can also use a repainted old ladder, which will give you the chance to custom-design a unique piece.

0866

0867

0868

0869

0870 The shelf under the long vanity accentuates the horizontality in this bathroom. It also echoes the fact that the bathroom floor is raised above the rest of the dwelling. Further, this horizontality is emphasized by the rows of white fabric containers.

0871 The space under the washbasin is a tempting spot for storing bathroom toiletries, or anything that cannot go anywhere else due to lack of space. Keep your eyes peeled for an appropriate piece of furniture that also looks good in your bathroom.

0872

0873

0874

0875

0876

0877

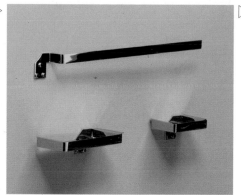

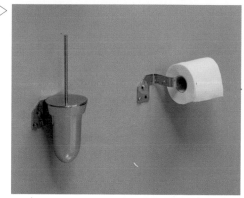

0878

0872 An otherwise bland bathroom is livened up with colorful accessories on the counter and a coat stand next to a light source, which makes the colors more vibrant. Also, the curvy lines of the coat stand contrast with the bathroom's linear style.

0873 A low cabinet under the sink fulfills the storage necessities of this open bathroom. Access to the valves is made easy. To hide the plumbing, two stainless steel towel bars are mounted on the front of the vanity.

0874 Vintage wire baskets are good to hold spare toilet paper rolls or any small items such as soap bars and lotions. They provide storage space and they are a great accent for the bathroom.

0875 Decorative stone and wood wall knob hooks add a natural accent to this bathroom. Rounded over time by rolling in the ocean, each stone is unique. Used in groups they have the quality of an art installation displayed on the wall.

0876 A combination of open shelf and drawer offers storage flexibility under the washbasin: An open shelf for easy access to hand towels and a drawer for toiletries to keep the area above the washbasin clutter-free.

0877 Toilets or washbasins in stainless steel are tempting, but this material can give a bathroom a cold, sterile feel when used in excess. Stainless steel accessories often acheive the right amount, providing a bathroom with a sleek look.

0878 Adding a towel bar to an existing vanity is easily done. Not only will this free up your countertop and walls, but in combination with other accessories including a toilet paper holder and hooks, they will round off your bathroom décor.

0879 The Butterfly chair, a classic designed by Jorge Ferrari-Hardoy in 1938, is popular for outdoor spaces. Its sturdy steel frame pairs nicely with fabric made from marine-grade acrylic, cotton or natural leather.

0880 Plastic outdoor furniture is waterproof, practical, durable and does not break the outdoor design budget. Powder-coated cast aluminum is a sturdier, yet still lightweight, alternative to plastic.

0881 A salvaged wood bench is transformed into a comfortable seat with the addition of cushions and pillows in varying patterns and colors. The bench brings a worldliness to the porch's decoration.

0882 Improvise a daybed by placing a large, firm cotton cushion directly on the ground. Complete the set with blankets and pillows of different sizes and patterns.

0883 When choosing throw pillows and fabrics to use on your porch, make sure they withstand UV rays, heat, water and inclement weather. Some suitable fabrics for outdoor use include various kinds of cotton, acrylic and other synthetic materials.

0884 You can make your outdoor space cozier with a daybed. Whether it is made of cast iron, wood or wicker, this hybrid piece of furniture works in many ways and was used by ancient Greek, Roman and Chinese cultures.

0885 This casual dining room with stone walls is light and airy. It opens up to a secluded patio furnished with lounge chairs and casual accessories, adding to the rustic charm of this country house.

0886 Folding metal furniture is ideal because it is compact, portable and versatile, allowing us to effortlessly change the mood of a space at a moment's notice.

0883

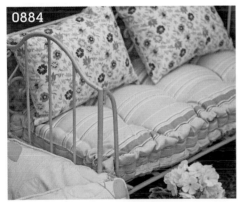

0884

0886

0885

0887 Treated natural wood is a suitable choice for a deck, but mixed materials are a perfectly acceptable alternative. A wide range of natural wood finishes and color options are available on the market, as well as outdoor furniture sets that are are designed specifically to combine well with wood.

0888 Eames' molded plastic RAR rocking chair adds a sophisticated feeling to any indoor or outdoor space. The curved edge of its seat reduces the pressure on the back of your thighs, making this a very comfortable seat.

0889 Powder-coated steel furniture is a good choice for everyday outdoor use, which requires durability and long-lasting beauty. Powder-coated finishes resist scratches and corrosion, making them ideal for all weather conditions.

0890 Weathered wood can be unsightly when it is not intentional, but if this is the look you are hoping to achieve, then weathered patinas can provide a rustic charm and complement any outdoor setting.

0887

0888

0889

0890

0891

0892

0893

0894

0891 A weathered blue-gray finish on wicker furniture and accessories is ideal for creating a nautical theme. The look is cool and relaxed, perfect for a beachside home.

0892 A clean, breezy and casual nautical style can be achieved by painting old wood furniture and accessories. Shades of white, green, blue and gray are always good choices. For a decorative touch, add pillows with matching fabrics and patterns.

0893 Wicker furniture is a popular choice for outdoor spaces as it creates a relaxed atmosphere, especially with cushioned seats. As far as style goes, choose whatever matches your home décor: classic, country or modern.

0894 Wrought iron furniture brings a touch of old-fashioned charm to your patio. In this daybed, the rigidity of the wrought iron is softened by its cushion and pillows in ocean-inspired tones.

0895 Rustic wicker and natural wood furniture are ideal for furnishing your casual beach house or your rustic cottage in the mountains.

0896 This iron chair has a woven plastic seat that is available in a range of colors. Its creative design is a modern interpretation of the traditional corded rope chair, which was made popular in the 1940s by furniture designer Hans Wegner.

0897 Canvas is heavy fabric woven from cotton, linen, hemp, jute or polyester. It is a good choice when resistance and durability are necessities in order to withstand varying weather conditions.

0898 Wicker is made of willow, reed or rattan. Being a natural material, it integrates well into casual, outdoor environments. It can also be stained or painted to add flair to your garden, patio or terrace.

0899 Portable furniture is ideal for a picnic or an afternoon tea outdoors because it is lightweight and easy to transport. Maneuverability is key, so any piece of furniture should fold to fit in the trunk of a car.

0895

0896

0897

0898

0899

0900

0901

0902

0903

0900 This version of the original Adirondack armchair, designed by Thomas Lee in 1903, maintains the main features of its predecessor: an angled back made from wooden boards and wide armrests that provide casual comfort. This piece of furniture is perfect for a cottage setting.

0901 This Tartaruga gazebo has a wooden structure and a white canvas covering to protect loungers from the sun. Enjoying a nice meal or drinks on a warm summer's day is made all the more enjoyable in this stylish gazebo.

0902 Nested side tables are usually sold in groups of two or three and come in handy for entertaining. They can be arranged in many ways, together or separately, and may even double as additional seats!

0903 This spacious, wooden gazebo serves as an outdoor room, with cushioned benches, side tables and planters — all under the protection of an awning to make the most of outdoor living.

0904 A gazebo is always a nice addition to a garden or backyard. Not only is it well-suited for entertaining friends and family throughout the year, it is an ideal hideaway space to enjoy a good book.

0905 This gray polyethylene sofa for Gervasoni's InOut collection is a take on the traditional wing chair. In an unusual twist, the wings on this chair extend all the way to the armrests. This modern interpretation, however, serves the same purpose as its predecessor, which is to provide protection from drafts.

0906 Designed especially for outdoor use, this daybed for Gervasoni's InOut collection is made of a woven polyethylene base and a polyurethane mattress.

0907 Cane and bamboo can be converted into sturdy and unique furniture, suitable for both traditional and contemporary designs.

0908

0909

0908 The chairs and tables in this Le Terrazze set can be configured in many different ways to suit the surrounding environment. These images show how natural wood furniture can be incorporated seamlessly into poolside settings.

0909 The design of the Adirondack chair offers a versatility that continues to meet modern design challenges. Many designers have adapted its classic form to contemporary settings. These teak lounge chairs by Gervasoni have adjustable backs and cushions that are available in various colors.

0910 The undulating shape of these cotton lounge chairs and side tables by Myyour are inspired by nature. Made of ABS translucent Plexiglas and painted metal, these pieces look like delicate leaves.

0911 Zoe, manufactured by Myyour, is an ergonomic lounge chair with an adjustable back that allows you to enjoy it in both a reclined and upright position. It comes in three finishes: embossed print, glossy paint or faux leather.

0912 A wooden pergola with a rectractable awning and screens on two sides creates a protected outdoor room. Just like any other room in your home, this space should convey personality through well-selected furniture, accessories and lighting.

0913 These lounge chairs by Tartaruga are protected from the sun, which means that there is no need for an umbrella. The result is a perfect example of "form follows function" made beautiful.

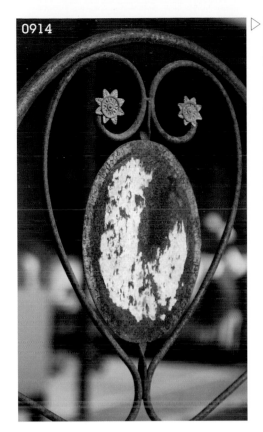

0914

0915

0916

0917

0914 Vintage, wrought iron furniture is a hot commodity for handicraft enthusiasts. They prefer the sturdiness and artistry that this material offers over similar products in cast aluminum that are much lighter and cheaper, but less charming.

0915 Resin wicker is used mainly for outdoor patio furniture. Unlike natural wicker or rattan, resin wicker is resistant against UV radiation and mildew and is therefore more durable.

0916 This Gervasoni line of armchairs, sofas and coffee tables in teak are ideal for a shady space brimming with vegetation. This line's simple design appears to be inspired by the Arts and Crafts movement.

0917 The casual canopy over this teak sofa will make a terrific addition to your garden or backyard. Light-filtering sheer fabric can be pulled around the sofa to create an airy, whimsical atmosphere.

0918

0919

0920

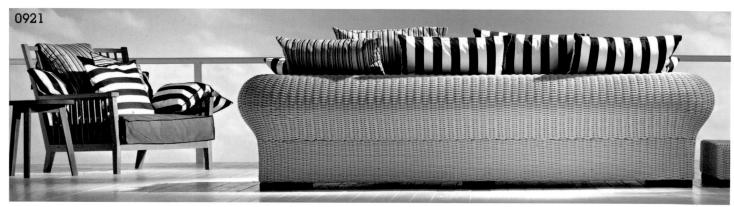

0921

0922

0923

0924

0925

0918 This sofa is deep enough that it can be used as a daybed. The extra pillows reduce the depth to that of a standard sofa, while bringing color and texture to the ensemble. Because of its slim frame, the sofa does not look bulky.

0919 The Cubetto sofa from Novo has a blockboard frame finished in different veneers. Because of its size, it will take center stage in a large living room or on a porch, well protected from the elements.

0920 This deep blue and crisp white outdoor furniture set looks bright and airy, embodying a chic Greek island vibe. Whitewashed walls and sparkling azure waters would make for a perfect backdrop.

0921 Blue and white striped fabrics add a nautical touch to your outdoor space. The wooden frame of this armchair interrupts the color scheme without transforming the overall atmosphere of the space.

0922 Gervasoni's refreshing version of the garden armchair has a malacca frame woven with white polyethylene, which creates an elegant Mediterranean style.

0923 Garden furniture can create a strong impact on the atmosphere of your outdoor event. To host a successful party, make sure you have some elegant yet comfortable outdoor furniture. You can make things interesting by assembling a variety of seats.

0924 Gervasoni's teak lounge chair has an adjustable slat back and roll cushion to combine style and function, bringing comfortable elegance to your outdoor patio, pool area or garden.

0925 The Sundance chair from Tonon is made of white polyethylene and is suitable for outdoor and indoor use. A sophisticated manufacturing process that uses rotational molding allows for the production of these high-quality, hollow and seamless objects.

0926 A well-protected porch can be the perfect setting for a casual summer dining area, reserving the dining room for formal events. If space allows, you may even have your special outdoor china displayed in a cabinet or sideboard.

0927 Chair decoration is usually overlooked, but with the right accessories you can transform a nondescript folding chair into a design statement for any type of event.

0928 A large, heavy table can remain as a permanent piece of furniture on your porch, while chairs and benches can be set up only when needed. In addition to freeing up much-needed space, this will allow the table to have multiple functions throughout the year.

0929 There are many ways to create attractive dining sets. One of them is to combine mismatched chairs and tables, lending visual texture to your outdoor space.

0930 A small, folding side table is a practical addition to any large gathering. Use it to serve snacks and drinks during a party, to hold serving dishes before a meal or to set aside used dishes while guests are still at the table.

0931 Foldable tables and chairs are very convenient for casual al fresco dining: they are easy to set up and just as easy to take down.

0932 A casual and eclectic selection of outdoor furniture on shady patios or gardens creates inviting places to linger on hot summer days. This seemingly effortless style is the signature characteristic of country decorating.

0933 Folding completely flat, the popular bistro table and chairs are certainly practical, especially when limited space is an issue.

0934 This solid and sturdy dining set goes well with any décor. It also contrasts nicely with this light, foldable, powder-coated table and chair, which in the occasion of a large gathering can come in handy as an additional surface.

0931

0932

0933

0934

0935 The clean and geometric design of this table, bench and chairs combine with the rustic materials of the porch, creating a unique contrast within this outdoor space.

0936 Practical and lightweight, folding metal furniture in different colors add some punch to your patio, backyard or terrace. For a refined look, combine with pillows and table sets in matching tones and patterns.

0937

0938

0939

0940

0937 Leaving wood untreated is rarely a consideration. Nonetheless, untreated wooden furniture integrates effectively into natural settings when paired with the right accessories.

0938 This stylish cast aluminum table with a tempered glass top and matching mesh chairs are perfect for summer days by the pool. Mesh chairs offer superior ventilation and therefore are a good choice for lounging on hot days.

0939 This table is made of zinc-plated iron with a Carrara marble tabletop. The silvery blue finish of the structure and its slim top provide a handsome contrast to the ivy-covered wall.

0940 A tumbled marble floor, brick walls, high ceilings and a large wooden door grace this entryway. This elegant setting, however, seems to overpower the diminutive dining table and chairs. When selecting furniture, ensure they harmonize with the style and the materials of the room in which they will be located.

0941

0942

0943

0944

0941 These built-in planters along a stone wall double as a long bench with a back rest. Pillows provide added comfort and touches of color.

0942 A ceramic border in blue, white and gold set into the terracotta flooring marks out a space for tables and chairs while leaving an accessible route around the pool.

0943 Similar to folding metal patio furniture, this line of table and chairs by Le Terrazze is practical by design. Wood adds a natural feel and a sturdiness without loosing the lightweight character so common in folding furniture.

0944 A large terrace may feel cold and unwelcoming before it is furnished and landscaped with planters and flower pots. To bring down the scale, a good idea is to divide the terrace into different areas. This image shows how different areas can be framed with canopies and plant urns.

0945 Le Terrazze proposes a line of dining tables and chairs that combines the modern and urban character of aluminum and glass with the warmth of wood and synthetic wicker.

0946 Add a special touch to untreated wood furniture to bring out the beauty of this natural material. A matching table runner and chair cushions in a muted brown color don't compete with the color and texture of the wood.

0947 This dining area is open to the garden while at the same time it occupies its own space. These separate areas are created by the cast iron structure of the canopy and the difference in the ground's material.

0948 This glass pitcher and cup add a little whimsy to the dining table with patterns that reflect the light in different ways. Their green tones echo the lush vegetation of the surroundings.

0949 Get inspired by the bright, sunny colors in your garden when you set your table for an outdoor meal. Decoration can be formal or casual, depending on the occasion and on the guests.

0950 Seasons are a good theme to use when decorating your table. In this image, earth tones, natural materials and small clusters of walnuts celebrate the fall, and leave behind bold, sunny colors that are more associated with warmer months.

0951 This practical picnic tray with handles and compartments helps keep everything in order: glasses, plates, silverware and even wine bottles.

0952 A tablecloth will hide a table that is not up to snuff and adds a touch of elegance to a special occasion. When your table is in good condition, however, you can forego a tablecloth and simply opt for placemats. They can easily be changed to reflect the season.

0953 If you are running low on ideas for table settings, look somewhere outside the ordinary: organic-shaped plates and bowls with delicate patterns.

0954

0955

0956

0957

0954 A white orchid in a square vase and a glass jar with a lid accent this chic table. The white and yellow colors of the orchid harmonize with the white-washed walls and blue chairs and windows.

0955 From simple groupings of flowers to elaborate floral arrangements, decorating with flowers will bring a fresh touch of color and energy to your table. Paying attention to details will make your tabletop very personal.

0956 Impress your guests with creative table settings for a brunch outdoors. Start with a design theme that is either casual or elegant, floral or striped, and apply it to all the items on the table.

0957 A picnic on a warm, sunny day is an excellent idea to celebrate the height of spring. Heavy fabrics, muted colors and drab tableware give way to brightly colored plastic glasses, pillows, blankets and wicker trays.

0958 This simple and functional floor lamp looks like a modern take on a hanging paper lamp. It emits a soft glow that adds ambiance to the room and makes a perfect reading lamp when positioned next to a chair.

0959 Look for knickknacks around your house and garden to create new objects, such as this lampshade with pebbles and salvaged glass decorations that once were part of a chandelier. All the pieces are tied to a thick wire spiral that is attached to a light cord wrapped in burlap fabric.

0960 If your porch is your favorite spot to read and write, find a task light that will suit the décor of this quiet area and will invite you to relax with a good book, or with a notebook and pen.

0961 Don't these lights look like artwork that artist Eva Hesse could have done? This unique and highly creative group of pear-shaped resin light fixtures is an example of the blurred line between design and art.

0962 Use unexpected materials like wire mesh and a sheet of wood veneer to create a unique and inexpensive ceiling light fixture. Of course, do not forget some basic light hardware!

0963 This fabulous handcrafted Moroccan-style lantern exudes elegance. Perfect for entry halls and porches, it adds an exotic touch with its elaborate star-shaped patterns and colored glass.

0964 Decorative lanterns come in many styles, colors and finishes. They are a popular item for outdoor decoration and add enchantment to summer evenings, whether ceiling or wall mounted, or simply set on the floor or on a piece of furniture.

0965 These outdoor floor lamps with white polyethylene shades make for delightful evenings out in the garden or by the pool. Their design goes well with the sinuous shape of the lounge chairs and the round side tables.

0962

0963

0964

0965

0969

0970

0971

0966 The Tulip XL outdoor lights by Myyour are both decorative and functional. The glowing tulips catch everyone's attention whether they are placed individually or set in groups as if they were growing out of a planter.

0967 The glowing lamp in this staged sitting area is not particularly suitable for outdoor use. However, worthy of note is the very clever effect achieved to simulate a sunset.

0968 In addition to providing general lighting, some ornamental light fixtures can highlight specific areas of your outdoor space. They can either take center stage or help demarcate boundaries and paths.

0969 Elsewhere we have seen a light fixture inspired by the sun, whereas this is one light design that looks more like the moon. In fact, it is one of the various items in this outdoor space that contributes to a circular theme.

0970 There is a growing number of designers interested in illuminated furniture. Functional as a bench and occasional table, this piece is also a light fixture with a fiberglass structure.

0971 The generous proportions of these polyethylene armchairs from the InOut collection by Gervasoni are perfect for relaxing outdoors in. A cover is available that can change the look of the chair completely.

0980 These all-white pieces of furniture and accessories add some zing to a weathered porch. A few decorative elements like flowers, a tarnished silver candle lantern and an off-white wool blanket soften the contrast.

0981 Old wicker-covered wine jugs and rusted metal urns are common decorative accents in cottage gardens. Lush vegetation and a seemingly unintentional placement of objects are key.

0982 Decorate your terrace with succulents in glass vases that are filled with colored sand for a simple and affordable decoration. Play around with varying arrangements, mixing different types of plants, sizes and colors.

0983 To decorate your countryside cabin, use colors that pay homage to the natural surroundings, like displaying a vintage basket full of freshly picked wild flowers. Modern items are not off limits. In fact, they can bring a sophisticated touch without looking out of place.

0984

0985

0986

0987

0984 Table centerpieces do not necessarily have to be grand. It all depends, of course, on the occasion. A casual yet elegant look can be achieved with a wildflower arrangement that echoes the natural surroundings.

0985 There's nothing better than a piece of wooden furniture to enhance the beauty of a natural backdrop. To keep wood furniture in good condition outdoors, soak it in oil a few times a year. This will help to keep the moisture out and protect it from the sun and wind as well.

0986 Woolen felt stones come in different sizes and shapes, just like the real thing. They can be used for seating and add a playful touch to playrooms. Not limited to indoor use, outdoor felt stones are treated with resin.

0987 Beach-themed decorations bring a calm and refreshing feel into your garden, whether you live in a tropical island or by the wild ocean of some northern country. Decorate with shells, driftwood and pebbles along with weathered and distressed finishes.

0988 Use colorful planters to liven up your garden. They are also great for breaking up an outdoor space into themed areas where planters are matched with plants according to color. You can also play with different heights to create attractive designs.

0989 Make your outdoor space as comfortable as your living room. A selection of casual and portable furniture and accessories is an easy way to create a cozy corner in the garden.

0990 A group of molded plastic armchairs and side tables counterbalances the rectangular shape of the pool. Their muted color harmonizes with the silvery green grasses, while the pillows and bright green decorations add refreshing touches.

0988

0989

0990

0991

0992

0993

0994

0991 Cut flowers placed in a pitcher on your desk by the window are cheerful. Match the tones of your flower arrangement with the color accents of the room and you'll have another element of décor!

0992 There are so many ways of recycling clutter to make fantastic decorative accents! Additionally, it's a good hobby to pick up. You decide how much time and effort you want to invest in your repurposing projects.

0993 Group vases of different sizes together for a greater effect and fill with plants, cut flowers or simply let them shine on their own. Keep in mind that bold patterns and saturated colors add visual weight and should therefore be used sparingly.

0994 Molded plastic outdoor furniture has many benefits: it is easy to clean, durable and lightweight. It is suitable if you have a big patio or backyard, but on the other hand, if your space is limited, you might not want to make this kind of investment, in which case simply opt for foldable furniture.

0995

0996

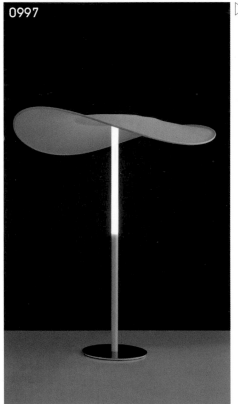

0997

0995 Transform your patio into an outdoor room where you can relax surrounded by plants. Just be patient: you are doing more than furnishing a room. Gardening is a work in progress that generally gets better every year. That is the beauty of it!

0996 Unless the patterns are subdued, avoid mixing more than three in one space. They do not have to be similarly themed. For instance, the curtain with a lighthouse design is combined with a solid, light-colored blanket with a blue fringe and thin-striped chair cushions and pillows.

0997 PO'light by jmferrero is the most sought-after item for hot days. At dusk it turns into a night umbrella with a light mast. With its integrated table, it becomes a pleasant gathering place for a small group.

0998 Copper accents add earthiness to this display. Even though the vases are a different color and material, they seem to blend easily with the ivy-covered wall thanks to their embossed surfaces. In fact, the result is quite homogeneous and very well balanced.

0999 Mixing fabrics, especially patterns, in one single space is not an easy task. Even in an open area, there is a risk of overdoing it. To start with, find a fabric you really like and work around it. You may choose from a selection of similar colors and patterns, which can be of different scales.

1000 Create an outdoor room with fabric as if it were a room in your house. The bushes and trees are the walls, and the lawn is the floor. Chairs and tables can be arranged the way you would arrange an indoor space, with pillows and accessories completing the look.

DIRECTORY

0001, 0004, 0005, 0007, 0008, 0009, 0010, 0014, 0015, 0016, 0017, 0018, 0021, 0022, 0026, 0028, 0029, 0030, 0031, 0033, 0034, 0035, 0036, 0037, 0042, 0043, 0045, 0046, 0047, 0048, 0049, 0050, 0056, 0066, 0067, 0068, 0069, 0070, 0071, 0072, 0073, 0074, 0075, 0076, 0077, 0078, 0079, 0080, 0081, 0082, 0083, 0084, 0085, 0086, 0087, 0088, 0089, 0090, 0091, 0092, 0093, 0094, 0095, 0096, 0097, 0098, 0099, 0100, 0101, 0102, 0104, 107, 0108, 0109, 0111, 0114, 0115, 0117, 0119, 0120, 0122, 123, 124, 125, 0127, 0129, 0131, 0132, 0133, 0134, 0135, 0136, 0138, 0139, 0140, 0141, 0142, 0143, 0145, 0146, 0147, 0148, 0149, 0150, 0159, 0160, 0161, 0162, 0163, 0164, 0165, 0166, 0168, 0169, 0170, 0171, 0172, 0173, 00174, 0175, 0181, 0191, 0192, 0193, 0195, 0205, 0206, 0207, 0208, 0209, 0210, 0211, 0212, 0213, 0214, 0215, 0216, 0218, 0219, 0220, 0222, 0223, 0224, 0225, 0226, 0227, 0228, 0229, 0232, 0234, 0237, 0238, 0240, 0241, 0242, 0243, 0244, 0246, 0247, 0248, 0249, 0250, 0251, 0252, 0253, 0254, 0255, 0256, 0261, 0268, 0269, 0270, 0271, 0272, 0273, 0274, 0275, 0277, 0279, 0280, 0283, 0284, 0285, 0292, 0293, 0294, 0295, 0307, 0311, 0312, 0313, 0315, 0316, 0318, 0320, 0321, 0322, 0324, 0326, 0327, 0328, 0330, 0331, 0334, 0342, 0347, 0356, 0372, 0373, 0374, 0375, 0376, 0377, 0378, 0379, 0380, 0381, 0382, 0385, 0388, 0389, 0391, 0394, 0396, 0398, 0399, 0402, 0403, 0404, 0405, 0406, 0407, 0409, 0410. 0411, 0412, 0415, 0416, 0453, 0454, 0459, 0460, 0467, 0473, 0474, 0478, 0479, 0480, 0481, 0482, 0485, 0486, 0487, 0488, 0489, 0490, 0492, 0493, 0494, 0515, 0516, 0517, 0518, 0519, 0520, 0521, 0523, 0524, 0525, 0526, 0527, 0528, 0531, 0532, 0534, 0537, 0541, 0542, 0548, 0549, 0550, 0551, 0552, 0553, 0554, 0555, 0557, 0558, 0560, 0562, 0563, 0564, 0567, 0568, 0569, 0570, 0571, 0572, 0573, 0574, 0575, 0577, 0579, 0581, 0582, 0584, 0585, 0586, 0587, 0588, 0590, 0593, 0594, 0603, 0604, 0605, 0606, 0607, 0608, 0609, 0610, 0611, 0612, 0613, 0614, 0615, 0616, 0617, 0618, 0619, 0620, 0621, 0622, 0623, 0624, 0625, 0626, 0627, 0628, 0629, 0630, 0631, 0632, 0633, 0634, 0637, 0649, 0651, 0653, 0654, 0656, 0657, 0659, 0668, 0669, 0670, 0671, 0672, 0673, 0674, 0675, 0676, 0677, 0678, 0679, 0680, 0681, 0682, 0683, 0684, 0685, 0686, 0688, 0689, 0690, 0693, 0694, 0695, 0696, 0697, 0700, 0701, 0702, 0703, 0704, 0706, 0708, 0709, 0712, 0713, 0716, 0721, 0723, 0726, 0731, 0732, 0733, 0736, 0737, 0739, 0742, 0743, 0746, 0747, 0748, 0749, 0750, 0751, 0752, 0758, 0759, 0760, 0761, 0762, 0763, 0764, 0765, 0774, 0776, 0780, 0783, 0785, 0790, 0791, 0792, 0793, 0794, 0795, 0796, 0797, 0798, 0799, 0801, 0802, 0804, 0805, 0806, 0808, 0809, 0810, 0811, 0812, 0813, 0814, 0815, 0816, 0817, 0818, 0819, 0820, 0821, 0822, 0823, 0824, 0826, 0827, 0828, 0829, 0830, 0831, 0832, 0833, 0834, 0836, 0839, 0840, 0842, 0845, 0846, 0850, 0853, 0855, 0859, 0860, 0861, 0862, 0863, 0864, 0865, 0866, 0867, 0868, 0869, 0870, 0871, 0872, 0873, 0874, 0875, 0876, 0878, 0879, 0880, 0881, 0882, 0884, 0885, 0886, 0887,

0888, 0889, 0890, 0891, 0892, 0893, 0894, 0895, 0896, 0897, 0898, 0899, 0900, 0902, 0914, 0926, 0927, 0928, 0929, 0930, 0931, 0932, 0933, 0934, 0935, 0936, 0937, 0938, 0946, 0948, 0949, 0950, 0951, 0952, 0953, 0956, 0957, 0959, 0960, 0962, 0963, 0964, 0974, 0975, 0976, 0977, 0978, 0979, 0980, 0981, 0982, 0983, 0984, 0985, 0986, 0987, 0989, 0991, 0992
© José Luis Hausmann
www.hausmannfotografia.com

0002
© Adrenalina
www.adrenalina.it

0003, 0004, 0011, 0013, 0020, 0023, 0024, 0040, 0052, 0058, 0063, 0113, 0233
© Arketipo
www.arketipo.com

0004 (0001)

0005 (0001)

0006, 0112, 0314
© Busnelli
www.busnelli.it

0007 (0001)

0008 (0001)

0009 (0001)

0010 (0001)

0011 (0003)

0012, 0033, 0053
© Blå Station
www.blastation.com

0013 (0003)

0014 (0001)

0015 (0001)

0016 (0001)

0017 (0001)

0018 (0001)

0019
© Divani&Divani
www.divaniedivani.it

0020 (0003)

0021 (0001)

0022 (0001)

0023 (0003)

0024 (0003)

0025 0031, 0039, 0051, 0332, 0335, 0336, 0371, 0561
© Bonaldo
www.bonaldo.it

0026 (0001)

0027 0110, 0348
© Casamilano
www.casamilanohome.com

0028 (0001)

0029 (0001)

0030 (0001)

0031 (0001)

0032 (0001)

0033 (0012)

0034 (0001)

0035 (0001)

0036 (0001)

0037 (0001)

0038
© Muuto
www.muuto.com

0039 (0025)

0040 (0003)

0041, 0055, 0064, 0105, 0151, 0344, 0602, 0636
© Minotti
www.minotti.com

0042 (0001)

0043 (0001)

0044, 0106, 0128
© Alivar
www.alivar.com

0045 (0001)

0046 (0001)

0047 (0001)

0048 (0001)

0049 (0001)

0050 (0001)

0051 (0025)

0052 (0003)

0053 (0012)

0054, 0262
© Carl Hansen & Son
http://www.carlhansen.com

0055 (0041)

0056 (0001)

0057 0278, 0319, 0546, 0666
© Marset
www.marset.com

0058 (0003)

0059, 0060, 0062, 0152, 0592, 0638
© Spinelli
www.fratellispinelli.it

0060 (0059)

0061, 0103, 0359
© Pierantonio Bonacina
www.pierantoniobonacina.it

0062 (0059)

0063 (0003)

0064 (0041)

0065, 0144, 0230, 0357, 0358, 0361, 0395, 0397, 0597
© Modà
www.modacollection.it

0066 (0001)

0067 (0001)

0068 (0001)

0069 (0001)

0070 (0001)

0071 (0001)

0072 (0001)

0073 (0001)

0074 (0001)

0075 (0001)

0076 (0001)

0077 (0001)

0078 (0001)

0079 (0001)

0080 (0001)

0081 (0001)

0082 (0001)

0083 (0001)

0084 (0001)

0085 (0001)

0086 (0001)

0087 (0001)

0088 (0001)

0089 (0001)

0090 (0001)

0091 (0001)

0092 (0001)

0093 (0001)

0094 (0001)

0095 (0001)

0096 (0001)

0097 (0001)

0098 (0001)

0099 (0001)

0100 (0001)

0101 (0001)

0102 (0001)

0103 (0061)

0104 (0001)

0105 (0041)

0106 (0044)

0107, 0116, 0153, 0154, 0155, 0368, 0641
© Besana
http://www.besana.it

0108 (0001)

0109 (0001)

0110 (0027)

0111 (0001)

0112 (0006)

0113 (0003)

0114 (0001)

0115 (0001)

0116 (0107)

0117 (0001)

0118
© AR.PA. Mobili
www.arpamobili.it

0119 (0001)

0120 (0001)

0121, 0130, 0591,
© Molteni&C
www.molteni.it

0122 (0001)

0123 (0001)

0124 (0001)

0125 (0001)

0126, 0156, 0353, 0589, 0635
© Mobili Bertelè
www.bertelemobili.it

0127 (0001)

0128 (0044)

0129 (0001)

0130 (0121)

0131 (0001)

0132 (0001)

0133 (0001)

0134 (0001)

0135 (0001)

0136 (0001)

0137, 0775, 0836, 0954
Herdade da Malhadinha
www.malhadinhanova.pt

0138 (0001)

0139 (0001)

0140 (0001)

0141 (0001)

0142 (0001)

0143 (0001)

0144 (0065)

0145 (0001)

0146 (0001)

0147 (0001)

0148 (0001)

0149 (0001)

0150 (0001)

0151 (0041)

0152 (0059)

0153 (0116)

0154 (0116)

0155 (0116)

0156 (0126)

0157, 0236
© Creazioni
www.stile-creazioni.com

0158, 0167, 0188, 0189, 0190, 0197, 0198,
0202, 0392, 0687, 0691, 0692, 0996, 0999,
1000
© Gancedo
www.gancedo.com

0159 (0001)

0160 (0001)

0161 (0001)

0162 (0001)

0163 (0001)

0164 (0001)

0165 (0001)

0166 (0001)

0167 (0158)

0168 (0001)

0169 (0001)

0170 (0001)

0171 (0001)

0172 (0001)

0173 (0001)

0174 (0001)

0175 (0001)

0176
© Harman Stoves
www.harmanstoves.com

0177, 0178, 0179, 0180, 0182, 0183, 0184,
0185, 0186, 0187, 0196, 0201, 0203, 0462,
0595, 0995
© MCZ spa
www.mcz.it

0178 (0177)

0179 (0177)

0180 (0177)

0181 (0001)

0182 (0177)

0183 (0177)

0184 (0177)

0185 (0177)

0186 (0177)

0187 (0177)

0188 (0158)

0189 (0158)

0190 (0158)

0191 (0001)

0192 (0001)

0193 (0001)

0194, 0310,
© Nemo Cassina
www.nemo.cassina.it

0195 (0001)

0196 (0177)

0197 (0158)

0198 (0158)

0199, 0204, 0239, 0343, 0345, 0346, 0354,
0365, 0384, 0386, 0387
© e15
www.e15.com

0200, 0352
© Doimo Idea
www.doimoidea.it

0201 (0177)

0202 (0158)

0203 (0177)

0204 (0199)

0205 (0001)

0206 (0001)

0207 (0001)

0208 (0001)

0209 (0001)

0210 (0001)

0211 (0001)

0212 (0001)

0213 (0001)

0214 (0001)

0215 (0001)

0216 (0001)

0217, 0281, 0305, 0306
© Ateljé Lyktan
www.atelje-lyktan.se

0218 (0001)

0219 (0001)

0220 (0001)

0221, 0351, 0383
© Ciacci Kreaty
http://www.ciacci.com

0222 (0001)

0223 (0001)

0224 (0001)

0225 (0001)

0226 (0001)

0227 (0001)

0228 (0001)

0229 (0001)

0230 (0065)

0231, 0235, 0393, 0400, 0598, 0600, 0601, 0700
© Noir
www.noir-italia.com

0232 (0001)

0233 (0003)

0234 (0001)

0235 (0231)

0236 (0157)

0237 (0001)

0238 (0001)

0239 (0199)

0240 (0001)

0241 (0001)

0242 (0001)

0243 (0001)

0244 (0001)

0245, 0580, 0583, 0883
© Coco-Mat
www.coco-mat.com

0246 (0001)

0247 (0001)

0248 (0001)

0249 (0001)

0250 (0001)

0251 (0001)

0252 (0001)

0253 (0001)

0254 (0001)

0255 (0001)

0256 (0001)

0257, 0297, 0652
© Vibia
www.vibia.com

0258
© Terzani
www.terzani.com

0259
© Axo Light
www.axolight.it

0260, 0655
© Catellani & Smith
www.catellanismith.com

0261 (0001)

0262 (0054)

0263, 0267, 0303,
© Steng Licht
www.steng.de

0264, 0289, 0296, 0545, 0958
© Louis Poulsen
www.louispoulsen.com

0265, 0276
© &Tradition
www.andtradition.com

0266
Occhio
www.occhio.de

0267 (0263)

0268 (0001)

0269 (0001)

0270 (0001)

0271 (0001)

0272 (0001)

0273 (0001)

0274 (0001)

0275 (0001)

0276 (0265)

0277 (0001)

0278 (0057)

0279 (0001)

0280 (0001)

0281 (0217)

0282
© Belux
www.belux.com

0283 (0001)

0284 (0001)

0285 (0001)

0286, 0970
© Prandina
www.prandina.it

0287
© Targetti
www.targetti.com

0288
© Atelier Areti
www.atelierareti.com

0289 (0264)

0290
© Next Lighting
www.nextlighting.com

0291
© Moooi
www.moooi.com

0292 (0001)

0293 (0001)

0294 (0001)

0295 (0001)

0296 (0264)

0297 (0257)

0298, 300, 0661, 0665
© LZF
www.lzf-lamps.com

0299, 0309
© Metalarte
http://www.metalarte.com

0300 (0298)

0301
Zeitlos Berlin
www.zeitlos-berlin.de

0302, 0304, 0325, 0547, 0658, 0664
© Lumini
www.lumini.com.br

0303 (0263)

0304 (0302)

0305 (0217)

0306 (0217)

0307 (0001)

0308
© Arturo Álvarez
www.arturo-alvarez.com

0309 (0299)

0310 (0194)

0311 (0001)

0312 (0001)

0313 (0001)

0314 (0006)

0315 (0001)

0316 (0001)

0317, 0544, 0667, 0845
© Trizo21
www.trizo21.com

0318 (0001)

0319 (0057)

0320 (0001)

0321 (0001)

0322 (0001)

0323
© Dluce
www.dluce.com

0324 (0001)

0325 (0302)

0326 (0001)

0327 (0001)

0328 (0001)

0329, 0543
© Light Years
www.lightyears.dk

0330 (0001)

0331 (0001)

0332 (0025)

0333, 0338, 0340, 0341, 0362, 0366
© Emmei
http://emmei.co.uk

0334 (0001)

0335 (0025, 599)

0336 (0025)

0337, 0350, 0390, 0596, 0646, 0699
© Jesse
www.jesse.it

0338 (0333)

0339, 0401, 0436, 0456, 0463, 0468, 0477,
0483, 0484, 0512, 0522, 0529, 0530, 0540
© Cesar
www.cesar.it

0340 (0333)

0341 (0333)

0342 (0001)

0343 (0199)

0344 (0041)

0345 (0199)

0346 (0199)

0347 (0001)

0348 (0027)

0349
© Elegance
www.elegancecy.com

0350 (0337)

0351 (0221)

0352 (0200)

0353 (0126)

0354 (0199)

0355, 0367, 0370, 0599
© Zanotta
www.zanotta.it

0356 (0001)

0357 (0065)

0358 (0065)

0359 (0061)

0360, 0660
© Leds-C4
www.leds-c4.com

0361 (0065)

0362 (0333)

0363, 0364
© Emmemobili
www.ommomobili.it

0364 (0363)

0365 (0199)

0366 (0333)

0367 (0355)

0368 (0107)

0369
© Oluce
www.oluce.com

0370 (0355)

0371 (0025)

0372 (0001)

0373 (0001)

0374 (0001)

0375 (0001)

0376 (0001)

0377 (0001)

0378 (0001)

0379 (0001)

0380 (0001)

0381 (0001)

0382 (0001)

0383 (0221)

0384 (0199)

0385 (0001)

0386 (0199)

0387 (0199)

0388 (0001)

0389 (0001)

0390 (0337)

0391 (0001)

0392 (0158)

0393 (0231)

0394 (0001)

0395 (0065)

0396 (0001)

0397 (0065)

0398 (0001)

0399 (0001)

0400 (0231)

0401 (0339)

0402 (0001)

0403 (0001)

0404 (0001)

0405 (0001)

0406 (0001)

0407 (0001)

0408, 0413, 0415, 0418, 0420, 0422, 0423,
0425, 0426, 0427, 0429, 0430, 0431, 0437,
0449, 0450, 0452, 0455, 0465, 0505, 0510,
0514, 0535, 0538
© Tecnocucina
www.tecnocucina.it

0409 (0001)

0410 (0001)

0411 (0001)

0412 (0001)

0413 (0408)

0414 (0001)

0415 (0408)

0416 (0001)

0417, 0424, 0438, 0439, 0440, 0441, 0442,
0443, 0445, 0447, 0448, 0451, 0466, 0476,
0491, 0498, 0508, 0511, 0513, 0533, 0539,
0556
© Dada
www.dadaweb.it

0418 (0408)

0419
© Bsweden
www.bsweden.com

0420 (0408)

0421, 0432, 0433, 0434, 0435, 0536
© Rational
www.rational-kitchens.com

0422 (0408)

0423 (0408)

0424 (0417)

0425 (0408)

0426 (0408)

0427 (408)

0428, 0457, 0458,
© Schiffini
www.schiffini.com

0429 (0408)

0430 (0408)

0431 (0408)

0432 (0421)

0433 (0421)

0434 (0421)

0435 (0421)

0436 (0339)

0437 (0408)

0438 (0417)

0439 (0417)

0440 (0417)

0441 (0417)

0442 (0417)

0443 (0417)

0444, 0446, 0464
© Mobalco
www.mobalco.com

0445 (0417)

0446 (0444)

0447 (0417)

0448 (0417)

0449 (0408)

0450 (0408)

0451 (0417)

0452 (0408)

0453 (0001)

0454 (0001)

0455 (0408)

0456 (0339)

0457 (0428)

0458 (0428)

0459 (0001)

0460 (0001)

0461
© Molo Design
http://molodesign.com

0462 (0177)

0463 (0339)

0464 (0444)

0465 (0408)

0466 (0417)

0467 (0001)

0468 (0339)

0469, 0470, 0471, 0472, 0475
© O&G
www.olivoegodeassi.it

0470 (0469)

0471 (0469)

0472 (0469)

0473 (0001)

0474 (0001)

0475 (0469)

0476 (0417)

0477 (0339)

0478 (0001)

0479 (0001)

0480 (0001)

0481 (0001)

0482 (0001)

0483 (0339)

0484 (0339)

0485 (0001)

0486 (0001)

0487 (0001)

0488 (0001)

0489 (0001)

0490 (0001)

0491 (0417)

0492 (0001)

0493 (0001)

0494 (0001)

0495, 0496, 0497, 0499, 0500, 0501, 0502, 0503, 0504, 0506, 0507, 0509
© Elica
www.elica.com

0496 (0495)

0497 (0495)

0498 (0417)

0499 (0495)

0500 (0495)

0501 (0495)

0502 (0495)

0503 (0495)

0504 (0495)

0505 (0408)

0506 (0495)

0507 (0495)

0508 (0417)

0509 (0495)

0510 (0408)

0511 (0417)

0512 (0339)

0513 (0417)

0514 (0408)

0515 (0001)

0516 (0001)

0517 (0001)

0518 (0001)

0519 (0001)

0520 (0001)

0521 (0001)

0522 (0339)

0523 (0001)

0524 (0001)

0525 (0001)

0526 (0001)

0527 (0001)

0528 (0001)

0529 (0339)

0530 (0339)

0531 (0001)

0532 (0001)

0533 (0417)

0534 (0001)

0535 (0408)

0536 (0421)

0537 (0001)

0538 (0408)

0539 (0417)

0540 (0339)

0541 (0001)

0542 (0001)

0543 (0329)

0544 (0317)

0545 (0264)

0546 (0057)

0547 (0302)

0548 (0001)

0549 (0001)

0550 (0001)

0551 (0001)

0552 (0001)

0553 (0001)

0554 (0001)

0555 (0001)

0556 (0417)

0557 (0001)

0558 (0001)

0559
© Iñaki Bergara
www.bergaraphoto.com

0560 (0001)

0561 (0025)

0562 (0001)

0563 (0001)

0564 (0001)

0565, 0566, 0576, 0578, 0640, 0643, 0644, 0645, 0698, 0705
© Cia International
www.ciainternational.it

0566 (0565)

0567 (0001)

0568 (0001)

0569 (0001)

0570 (0001)

0571 (0001)

0572 (0001)

0573 (0001)

0574 (0001)

0575 (0001)

0576 (0565)

0577 (0001)

0578 (0565)

0579 (0001)

0580 (0245)

0581 (0001)

0582 (0001)

0583 (0245)

0584 (0001)

0585 (0001)

0586 (0001)

0587 (0001)

0588 (0001)

0589 (0126)

0590 (0001)

0591 (0121)

0592 (0059)

0593 (0001)

0594 (0001)

0595 (0177)

0596 (0337)

0597 (0065)

0598 (0231)

0599 (0355)

0600 (0231)

0601 (0231)

0602 (0041)

0603 (0001)

0604 (0001)

0605 (0001)

0606 (0001)

0607 (0001)

0608 (0001)

0609 (0001)

0610 (0001)

0611 (0001)

0612 (0001)

0613 (0001)

0614 (0001)

0615 (0001)

0616 (0001)

0617 (0001)

0618 (0001)

0619 (0001)

0620 (0001)

0621 (0001)

0622 (0001)

0623 (0001)

0624 (0001)

0625 (0001)

0626 (0001)

0627 (0001)

0628 (0001)

0629 (0001)

0630 (0001)

0631 (0001)

0632 (0001)

0633 (0001)

0634 (0001)

0635 (0126)

0636 (0041)

0637 (0001)

0638 (0059)

0639, 0784, 0786, 0788, 0807, 0838, 0844,
0848, 0849, 0850, 0855, 0858, 0859
© Burgbad
http://burgbad.de

0640 (0565)

0641 (0107)

0642
© Lema
www.lemamobili.com

0643 (0565)

0644 (0565)

0645 (0565)

0646 (0337)

0647
© Flou
www.flou.it

0648
© Porro
www.porro.com

0649 (0001)

0650
© Former
www.former.it

0651 (0001)

0652 (0257)

0653 (0001)

0654 (0001)

0655 (0260)

0656 (0001)

0657 (0001)

0658 (0302)

0659 (0001)

0660 (0360)

0661 (0298)

0662
© Tobias Grau
www.tobias-grau.com

0663, 0965
© Lucente
www.lucente.eu

0664 (0302)

0665 (0298)

0666 (0057)

0667 (0317)

0668 (0001)

0669 (0001)

0670 (0001)

0671 (0001)

0672 (0001)

0673 (0001)

0674 (0001)

0675 (0001)

0676 (0001)

0677 (0001)

0678 (0001)

0679 (0001)

0680 (0001)

0681 (0001)

0682 (0001)

0683 (0001)

0684 (0001)

0685 (0001)

0686 (0001)

0687 (0158)

0688 (0001)

0689 (0001)

0690 (0001)

0691 (0158)

0692 (0158)

0693 (0001)

0694 (0001)

0695 (0001)

0696 (0001)

0697 (0001)

0698 (0565)

0699 (0337)

0700 (0231)

0701 (0001)

0702 (0001)

0703 (0001)

0704 (0001)

0705 (0565)

0706 (0001)

0707
© RES4
http://re4a.com

0708 (0001)

0709 (0001)

0710, 0711, 0714, 0715, 0717, 0718, 0719,
0722, 0725, 0727, 0728, 0729, 0730, 0734,
0735, 0738, 0740, 0741, 0745
© Dearkids
www.dearkids.lt

0711 (0710)

0712 (0001)

0713 (0001)

0714 (0710)

0715 (0710)

0716 (0001)

0717 (0710)

0718 (0710)

0719 (0710)

0720, 0724
© P'kolino
www.pkolino.com

0721 (0001)

0722 (0710)

0723 (0001)

0724 (0720)

0725 (0710)

0726 (0001)

0727 (0710)

0728 (0710)

0729 (0710)

0730 (0710)

0731 (0001)

0732 (0001)

0733 (0001)

0734 (0710)

0735 (0710)

0736 (0001)

0737 (0001)

0738 (0710)

0739 (0001)

0740 (0710)

0741 (0710)

0742 (0001)

0743 (0001)

0744
© Kinderräume
www.kinderraeume.com

0745 (0710)

0746 (0001)

0747 (0001)

0748 (0001)

0749 (0001)

0750 (0001)

0751 (0001)

0752 (0001)

0753
Slide
http://slidedesign.it

0754
© Less n more
www.less-n-more.com

0755, 0756
© Vertigo Bird
www.vertigo-bird.com

0756 (0755)

0757
© Carretero Design
www.carreterodesign.com

0758 (0001)

0759 (0001)

0760 (0001)

0761 (0001)

0762 (0001)

0763 (0001)

0764 (0001)

0765 (0001)

0766, 0771, 0773, 0863
© Hansgrohe International
www.hansgrohe-int.com

0767, 0789
© Barasona
http://barasona.com

0768, 770, 0772, 0777, 0778, 0779, 0781,
0782, 0803, 0852, 0853, 0857, 0877
© Rapsel
www.rapsel.it

0769
© Dornbracht
www.dornbracht.com

0770 (0768)

0771 (0766)

0772 (0768)

0773 (0766)

0774 (0001)

0775 (0137)

0776 (0001)

0777 (0768)

0778 (0768)

0779 (0768)

0780 (0001)

0781 (0768)

0782 (0768)

0783 (0001)

0784 (0639)

0785 (0001)

0786 (0639)

0787, 0825
© Alape
www.alape.com

0788 (0639)

0789 (0767)

0790 (0001)

0791 (0001)

0792 (0001)

0793 (0001)

0794 (0001)

0795 (0001)

0796 (0001)

0797 (0001)

0798 (0001)

0799 (0001)

0800
© Autoban
www.autoban212.com

0801 (0001)

0802 (0001)

0803 (0768)

0804 (0001)

0805 (0001)

0806 (0001)

0807 (0639)

0808 (0001)

0809 (0001)

0810 (0001)

0811 (0001)

0812 (0001)

0813 (0001)

0814 (0001)

0815 (0001)

0816 (0001)

0817 (0001)

0818 (0001)

0819 (0001)

0820 (0001)

0821 (0001)

0822 (0001)

0823 (0001)

0824 (0001)

0825 (0787)

0826 (0001)

0827 (0001)

0828 (0001)

0829 (0001)

0830 (0001)

0831 (0001)

0832 (0001)

0833 (0001)

0834 (0001)

0835 (0001)

0836 (0137)

0837 (0001)

0838 (0639)

0839 (0001)

0840 (0001)

0841 (0001)

0842
© Tervhivatal
www.tervhivatal.hu

0843 (0001)

0844 (0639)

0845 (0317)

0846 (0001)

0847 (0001)

0848 (0639)

0849 (0639)

0850 (0639)

0851 (0001)

0852 (0768)

0853 (0768)

0854 (0001)

0855 (0639)

0856 (0001)

0857 (0768)

0858 (0639)

0859 (0639)

0860 (0001)

0861 (0001)

0862 (0001)

0863 (0766)

0864 (0001)

0865 (0001)

0866 (0001)

0867 (0001)

0868 (0001)

0869 (0001)

0870 (0001)

0871 (0001)

0872 (0001)

0873 (0001)

0874 (0001)

0875 (0001)

0876 (0001)

0877 (0768)

0878 (0001)

0879 (0001)

0880 (0001)

0881 (0001)

0883 (0245)

0884 (0001)

0885 (0001)

0886 (0001)

0887 (0001)

0888 (0001)

0889 (0001)

0890 (0001)

0091 (0001)

0892 (0001)

0893 (0001)

0894 (0001)

0895 (0001)

0896 (0001)

0897 (0001)

0898 (0001)

0899 (0001)

0900 (0001)

0901, 0903, 0904, 0908, 0912, 0913, 0915, 0940, 0941, 0942, 0943, 0944, 0945, 0947, 0955, 0961, 0988
© Pircher
www.pircher.eu

0902 (0001)

0903 (0901)

0904 (0901)

0905, 0906, 0907, 0909, 0916, 0917, 0918, 0920, 0921, 0922, 0923, 0924, 0939, 0971, 0990, 0993, 0994, 0998
© Gervasoni
www.gervasoni1882.it

0906 (0905)

0907 (0905)

0908 (0901)

0909 (0905)

0910, 0911, 0966, 0968, 0969
© Myyour
www.myyour.eu/it

0911 (0910)

0912 (0901)

0913 (0901)

0914 (0001)

0915 (0901)

0916 (0905)

0917 (0905)

0918 (0905)

0919
© Novo Design
www.novoitalia.it

0920 (0905)

0921 (0905)

0922 (0905)

0923 (0905)

0924 (0905)

0925
© Tonon
www.tononitalia.com

0926 (0001)

0927 (0001)

0928 (0001)

0929 (0001)

0930 (0001)

0931 (0001)

0932 (0001)

0933 (0001)

0934 (0001)

0935 (0001)

0936 (0001)

0937 (0001)

0938 (0001)

0939 (0905)

0940 (0901)

0941 (0901)

0942 (0901)

0943 (0901)

0944 (0901)

0945 (0901)

0946 (0001)

0947 (0901)

0948 (0001)

0949 (0001)

0950 (0001)

0951 (0001)

0952 (0001)

0953 (0001)

0954 (0137)

0955 (0901)

0956 (0001)

0957 (0001)

0958 (0264)

0959 (0001)

0960 (0001)

0961 (0901)

0962 (0001)

0963 (0001)

0964 (0001)

0965 (0663)

0966 (0910)

0967
© Royal Botania
www.royalbotania.com

0968 (0910)

0969 (0910)

0970 (0286)

0971 (0905)

0972, 0973
© Shades of Green Landscape Architecture
www.shadesofgreenla.com

0973 (0972)

0974 (0001)

0975 (0001)

0976 (0001)

0977 (0001)

0978 (0001)

0979 (0001)

0980 (0001)

0981 (0001)

0982 (0001)

0983 (0001)

0984 (0001)

0985 (0001)

0986 (0001)

0987 (0001)

0988 (0901)

0989 (0001)

0990 (0905)

0991 (0001)

0992 (0001)

0993 (0905)

0994 (0905)

0995 (0177)

0996 (0158)

0997
© Punt Mobles
www.puntmobles.com

0998 (0905)

0999 (0158)

1000 (0158)